Rebuilding Blockley

The story of how the talented surveyor Oliver Dicks helped redesign and refurbish well over 100 properties in the Blockley vicinity.

Published in memory of Oliver Dicks
by the Blockley Heritage Society, Malvern Mill, Blockley GL56 9HA
(incorporated in England as a company limited by guarantee number 7008626 and registered as a charity number 1133319)
with financial assistance from The Abacus Charitable Trust.
© Copyright Blockley Heritage Society 2010
ISBN 978-0-9563738-1-6
British Library Cataloguing in Publication Data:
A catalogue record for this book is available from the British Library

Proceeds from the sale of this book will contribute to the cost of building the Blockley Community Heritage Centre

Printed and bound in the UK by the MPG Books Group, Bodmin and King's Lynn.

Contents

Acknowledgements

A book of this nature could not be produced without a lot of help from many sources. In particular I would like to record my appreciation to the following:

- Jean Dicks for granting access to Oliver's computer and permission to reproduce his drawings, for her recollections, for her patience and for many cups of tea. Kate Dicks for her additional input and support;
- All of the Blockley property owners (past and present) who so readily gave their time, their recollections, their photographs and their drawings without which this book would have been very thin indeed;
- Simon Bolton for many recollections of the times he worked on building projects designed by Oliver;
- Paul Adams and Jeremy Bourne for reviewing the text both for grammatical correctness and historical accuracy;
- Tony Skellett, Gay Thompson, Keyna Doran, and Rob and Gill Greenstock for the use of their photographs;
- John Malin and The Corinium Museum for the provision of historical photographs;
- Sharan and Johnty Stoker for use of the photograph of Oliver Dicks on page 9;
- Alan Bennett for permission to use his firm's architectural drawings of *The Crown Inn;*
- Colin Threadgill for help in interrogating Oliver's computer filing system;
- Cotswold District Council and Gloucestershire County Archives for access to their records;

and anyone else who has contributed to this work and who accidentally may have been overlooked.

Robert Willott
July 2010

Foreword

By Jeremy Bourne
Chairman of the Blockley Heritage Society

For Blockley Heritage Society, it is a privilege and a pleasure to be the publishers of this account of the life and work of Oliver Dicks. Oliver was a true son of Blockley. He understood completely the historical and architectural importance of this unique Cotswold village.

Blockley has a long and unusual history. Our valley was first settled more than 1200 years ago, and the footprint of the central village has altered little in all that time. The huddled buildings that form the High Street and the area round the Church present an intriguing challenge to the architect and surveyor. Built in the late 16th, 17th and 18th centuries using locally quarried Cotswold stone and hand-cut stone tiles, the houses nevertheless have the air of a northern industrial village. Indeed, for two centuries, Blockley was an industrial town supported by the silk industries and based on its string of watermills along the fast-running brook.

Oliver was able, to an extraordinary degree, to distinguish the different architectural elements within this community. He knew which dormers, string courses, dripstones or paving slabs were an essential part of the Blockley and Cotswold historical style. But he also understood the peculiar geology of the Jurassic limestone and clay beds, which can so treacherously cause buildings to slide. He knew which designs, both artistic and engineering, might cause trouble with planning inspectors, and which ones would be seen as uncontroversial. Yet he was not a dogmatic conservationist. Even if passionate about the Blockley heritage, he was not afraid to recommend bold and modern solutions when he felt they were suitable. In handling both his clients and the local authorities, he knew when to be utterly charming and persuasive, and when to be resolute, even fierce, in standing his ground over an issue which he believed to be important.

But hand in hand with his detailed professional knowledge, there went a tremendous sense of community, of empathy with his many Blockley friends and their needs. Pubs and parties, with all the personal friendships made there, were of real importance to him, and partly explain why he was so successful in carrying along with him both his clients and the authorities. He was also astonishingly generous with his time and advice, and we read again and again in this book how difficult his friends found it to reward him for all that he did for them.

The Society and everyone who loves the Blockley scene will be hugely grateful to Robert Willott for undertaking this account of Ollie's life and work in Blockley. The book will remain as a treasure for long years to come. But so will the many rescued houses and restoration projects that Ollie has left us. As was written of another great British building designer: "If you want a monument, look around you."

Jeremy Bourne,
Chairman,
Blockley Heritage Society
14 July 2010

CHAPTER 1

Oliver Dicks

*"I first met Oliver exactly 13 years ago when I moved to Blockley. After a couple of days I
thought I would at least give The Great Western Arms a try. There was Ollie. He said
'hello' and made me feel welcome and I feel he has been a friend ever since."*

With these words Peter Mansion opened a tribute to Oliver Dicks at his funeral on Friday 5 November 2008. Peter's was an experience shared by many newcomers to Blockley, a fair proportion of whom had two urgent priorities to address on their arrival. First there was the social need to meet fellow residents, and no-one has yet found a much better way to do that than by sharing a pint in the local pub. Secondly, there was almost inevitably the need to reconfigure and/or refurbish the property that each had just acquired. In Oliver they found one man who could satisfy both needs, and who readily did so.

No wonder so many people queued to attend his funeral, some having to stand in the packed Oakley Wood Crematorium to show their appreciation of his life and to pay their last respects.

Oliver was the son of George and Olwen Dicks, born at Edgbaston, Birmingham, on 20 September 1943. George Dicks ran a bakery business and was already in his fifties when Oliver was born. At the age of seven Oliver was sent to board at Rydal School in Colwyn Bay and for most of his years thereafter the family home was to be a place that Oliver would visit rather than reside in. As a Rydal pupil he excelled at most sports, including rugby, gymnastics and golf. Doubtless it was there also that Oliver developed the independent - some would say stubborn - streak in his character.

After Rydal, Oliver continued his studies at the Royal Agricultural College, Cirencester. By then his parents had retired and moved away from Edgbaston to buy a disused silk mill in Blockley known as Sleepy Hollow together with part of the spinney on the other side of the Draycott road.

Oliver left college at Cirencester to train as a land agent and chartered surveyor in Norfolk. Then he took an estate management job in Ross-on-Wye before moving on to work for an architectural practice in Stourbridge - some 40 miles or so from his parents' new home. Oliver was now able to spend more time in and around Blockley and was soon pursuing his love of golf at Broadway Golf Club. He became a member of the club and remained so for the rest of his life, making a significant contribution to the development of its premises during that time.

Adjacent to the golf course is the Dormy House Hotel where Oliver was a frequent visitor and where he was to meet his wife Jean. In 1968 they married and in the same year Oliver joined the planning department of Evesham Borough Council. Also in 1968, Oliver and Jean bought the Bantam Tea Rooms business in Chipping Campden with help from his family, which Jean then managed. It provided them with a home for the next three years while Oliver developed his career in local government.

As a young man Oliver's sporting interests expanded into motor racing. He understood everything one could wish to know about the mechanical components of almost every motor car. Open top fast sports cars were his passion and Jean still remembers trips to race meetings in a converted old ambulance.

In 1974 a local government reorganisation resulted in Evesham Council's planning department being moved to the newly formed Wychavon District Council in Pershore where Oliver held the position of a building inspector. Always curious, quick to learn and with an elephantine memory, Oliver was soon accumulating the type of knowledge that would equip him to advise others about their building ambitions. "He had a real thirst for knowledge", Jean says, citing his love of quizzes and more recently his addiction to Sudoku.

As a building inspector, Oliver gained a reputation for attention to detail and for prudence. Often he would demand that foundations were made deeper than architects and builders might have wished. Before long he had earned the nickname of "One Foot Deeper Dicks".

Meanwhile family life at Sleepy Hollow had suffered a sad loss. Oliver's father George died in November 1970 and shortly afterwards his mother partitioned the garden to enable a new split level house to be built there for her. Oliver was not involved in the design, but occasionally found it difficult to restrain himself from expressing opinions to his mother about it.

Once the new house had been completed, Sleepy Hollow was sold to Sir Robert Lusty who changed the name to The Old Silk Mill. This enabled Olwen Dicks to retain the Sleepy Hollow name for her new home. A few years later Oliver and Jean moved back in with Olwen and Jean gave birth to their only daughter Kate there. Also during this period the spinney on the opposite side of the Draycott road was sold for development as The Dell.

In 1980 Oliver, Jean and Kate moved out of the new version of Sleepy Hollow (since renamed Brookwood) into Northwick Terrace. Shortly afterwards Oliver's mother moved to Vale Cottage at the Dovedale end of the High Street, alongside the same Blockley Brook that she would have previously watched flowing swiftly into the Sleepy Hollow mill pond further downstream. Eventually Oliver would inherit this property and embark on a complete refurbishment before making it his final family home[1].

Oliver's desire to use his ever expanding knowledge of building design and construction found expression initially in providing building advice and draw-

Below:
Oliver takes a look at the refurbishment of his
final home Vale Cottage

ings for a few acquaintances -always outside the Worcestershire planning region to avoid any conflict of interests. Some of his first drawing assignments were for a local developer Harold da Silva, such as the extension to Brambles - what Oliver described as "the best view in Blockley" - for Tom and Valerie Coombs.

With such an interest in buildings, it is hardly surprising that one of Oliver's favourite holidays was a cruise on the River Nile, not so much for the waterway but more to satisfy his interest in Egyptian ruins. According to his good friend John Dewhurst, Oliver was always up early so that he could get to the ruins before the temperature became too hot.

Nearer home he was also fascinated by the design and construction of Castle Drogo in Devon, created by Edwin Lutyens for the founder of Home & Colonial Stores and built as recently as 1930. Such was his interest that Oliver would spend time studying the building techniques involved and poring over a model displayed in the basement.

As the years went by Oliver increasingly found that his council work was wearing him down and his enthusiasm for it diminished. By contrast his enthusiasm for designing buildings and alterations was increasing exponentially. So in 1994 he took early retirement and quickly found himself immersed in helping all-comers with their building projects. His contribution was never influenced by the stature of the project or of its owner, but by whether he liked the person and was sympathetic to the project. He was as ready to submit plans for a greenhouse as he was to design a disabled access ramp for the Blockley Sports & Social Club.

Imaginative and impatient, honourable and practical, Oliver was generous with his time and talents, had a good sense of humour and enjoyed good company. He was not a man to suffer fools gladly, but he never bore a grudge.

When approached during his lifetime about the idea of collaborating on a book like this, Oliver was initially hesitant although he eventually agreed it would be an interesting project. However, he would probably have been embarrassed by its appearance, such was the underlying modesty of the man.

Any outsider would have been astonished to find someone willing to devote so much time and almost boyish enthusiasm to property projects without any expectation of financial reward. It was as if Oliver was running a one-man philanthropic building consultancy that over time helped upgrade, and thereby preserve from gradual decay, much of Blockley village.

It is to that work, described more fully in the chapters that follow, and to that very special man, that this book is dedicated.

CHAPTER 2

Blockley before the Dicks Makeover

"The High Street would cease to be the home of trades people and instead become the home of 'incomers'. Throughout the village these incomers would be buying up former shops, mills, pubs and houses."

In the early nineteen eighties Blockley was undergoing considerable change. The economics of village life were being transformed as supermarkets eroded the traditional role of the village shop. The widespread growth in car ownership was also playing its part in turning most village shops into optional extras where once they had been absolute necessities.

Local employment opportunities had already declined as farming became more mechanised. Some artisans were also being squeezed out of business by factory machinery. The impending closure of most of the remaining village shops threatened to reduce still further the number of local jobs available, despite the development of new opportunities at the nearby Northwick and Draycott business parks.

By 1981 roughly 50% of Blockley's population travelled out of the parish by car to work and a further 14% went to work beyond the Cotswold District by public transport[2].

Imagine walking along Bell Lane and the High Street in 1981 starting at the old Coach House. On the opposite side of the road was a general store and Post Office run by Jenny and Tony Davey. A few yards further uphill on the left was the Blockley Cobbler and then, on the corner of The Square leading down to the church, was Alec and Mary Graham's newsagents and greengrocery shop, followed by a branch of the Midland Bank and a small pharmacy.

Proceeding along the High Street, past an antiques shop on the left, one quickly came to the Balhatchet retail empire. On the left was Dashwood Balhatchet's ironmongery store (now Allcroft House) and beyond that Pauline Balhatchet ran the Wool Shop. Opposite was the popular butcher's shop and

Below:
Blockley High Street around 1980

The Square, Blockley.

greengrocery run by Maurice Balhatchet (the refurbished private residence still bears his name today). A little further on, just beyond School Lane, Jill Murray had a small gift shop on the right-hand side now known as Jasmine Cottage. There was no other shop, apart from Rochford's general store in Station Road opposite the Winterway junction. But the village still offered a choice of banks as Lloyd's occupied the building at the southwest end of what is now *The Crown Inn.*

Of those 11 retail businesses that had survived until 1981, most would soon wither away. The High Street (see plan) ceased to be the home of trades people and instead became the home of "incomers". Throughout the village these incomers were buying up former shops, mills, pubs and houses. As they did so, many properties would be refurbished and become the principal residence of their new owners. Others would be rented out to "weekenders" or used simply as a second home. New money would replace old, but the refurbished village would survive and even thrive.

By the time Oliver Dicks took early retirement in 1994 Blockley had already become a retail desert and so he was not involved to any material extent in the initial conversion of shops into private residences. However, as we shall see, he did play a significant role in redesigning parts of *The Crown* when it expanded into the adjacent premises vacated by Lloyd's Bank.

The impact of the village's economic decline had spread far beyond its shops so that many other properties were also in an outdated condition. It was in these other old properties that many of the incomers invested their new money and then turned to Oliver for help.

Above:
(Left) Lloyds Bank branch in part of what is now The Crown Inn.
(Right) Alec & Mary Graham's shop and the Midland Bank branch in The Square.
Opposite page:
Plan of Blockley village late in the 20th century showing (highlighted in red and blue) those properties where Oliver Dicks is known to have had an involvement .
© Crown Copyright 2009.

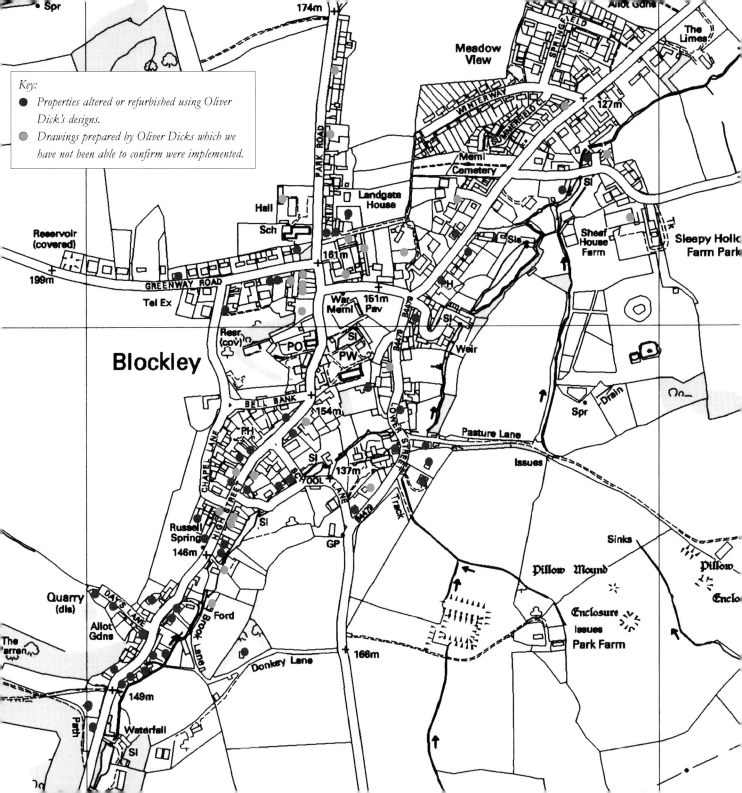

Key:
- **●** Properties altered or refurbished using Oliver Dick's designs.
- **●** Drawings prepared by Oliver Dicks which we have not been able to confirm were implemented.

Blockley

CHAPTER 3

Houses of Historic Interest

"I asked Ollie for a view on whether we would be completely
mad to buy it." The answer was characteristically direct:
"You've got to buy it!"

Opposite page:
Rock Cottage today with conservatory, bedroom
and kitchen extension on the left.
Below:
Mocking cartoon of former Rock Cottage
resident and prophetess Joanna Southcott
exposing herself to three physicians in order to
validate her pregnancy as the bearer of the
Second Messiah.

Rock Cottage stands proudly above Blockley High Street, with a formal pillared entrance to a drive that sweeps up from the road. Alongside the drive there is a pedestrian tunnel to the front door. The property was once owned by the Bishop of Worcester and in 1804 it became the home of the prophetess Joanna Southcott. In July 1971 it was gutted when the elderly owner Mrs Veysey-Stitt absent-mindedly poured paraffin on to an electric imitation coal fire[3].

The property was then bought and restored by two gentlemen Terry Hudson and Pat Litchfield. It was classified as a Grade II listed building of special architectural and historic interest.

In about 1989 Peter and Sally Jackson bought a property on the outskirts of Blockley as a second home while they searched for something more substantial to acquire as their permanent residence when they retired. A year or two later their attention was drawn to Rock Cottage by estate agents Jackson-Stops & Staff whose literature described the property as "a listed cottage residence of great character in an exotic garden setting". Almost inevitably Peter Jackson had by then met Oliver Dicks in the *Great Western Arms* and he invited Oliver to take a look at Rock Cottage for him: "I asked Ollie for a view on whether we would be completely mad to buy it." The answer was characteristically direct: "You've got to buy it!"

The Jacksons were impressed by Oliver's "wonderful vision" of what he could do with the property. Although it had been restored after the fire, it already had a dated appearance that was made worse by the extensive use of black paint and blue carpeting throughout. Soon Oliver was preparing drawings although he still had a full-time day job with Wychavon District Council. "He

Above:
Rock Cottage after Mrs Veysey-Stitt had
accidently set it on fire.

Below:
Rock Cottage restored after the fire as it
appeared immediately before purchase by Peter
and Sally Jackson .

was very reliable, always delivering on the due date", recalls Peter Jackson who also still had a full-time day job as managing director of a plastics machinery company based in Rugby.

The upgrading of the property included adding a conservatory and new kitchen on the first floor with a bedroom and bathroom above, all to the southwest of the existing building. A garage was also built at the opposite end, above which a guest room was added some five years later. On the lower ground floor the existing cloistered archways were enclosed with windows and a new front doorway and entrance hall were installed. In Sally Jackson's view, Oliver "changed the house dramatically".

The most evident original architectural feature of the property was the unusual and distinctive shape of the windows. They have a resemblance to a style sometimes found in the Middle East (see illustrations opposite). Oliver applied that same style not only to the new conservatory windows but also to the bannister balustrades on the staircase. The Jacksons don't recall having any disagreement with Oliver about his design ideas. Indeed Peter Jackson was moved to enquire why Oliver hadn't gone into property design earlier instead of working for Wychavon.

The planning approval process went through comparatively smoothly in 1992. There was one anxious moment when the planners thought the conservatory would be more acceptable if the woodwork was painted white. Sally Jackson thought it would have stood out "like a sore thumb", especially as all the existing shutters were stained dark green. Eventually the planners agreed.

Everyone in the Cotswolds has a favourite story about planners and the one that Sally Jackson tells involved a very formal meeting between the planning officer, Oliver Dicks and themselves. "The planning officer seemed a dry old stick", Sally recalls. "At the end of the meeting he stood up, shook Oliver's hand and said to him 'Thank you very much Mr Cox'. We managed to avoid crying with laughter until he had left!"

Oliver gave a huge amount of time to the project - far more than he had bargained for, as the contractors Birchway Builders went bust in the middle of the contract. Lawyers produced paperwork specifying what the Jacksons owed for the work completed to date and, while both Oliver and Peter were at work, Sally was saddled with the task of handing over a cheque - but only after Birchway's owner Bill Butterworth had signed an undertaking that the payment represented a final settlement of all obligations towards him. Butterworth then went outside to his staff, announced the company had closed and fired them on the spot.

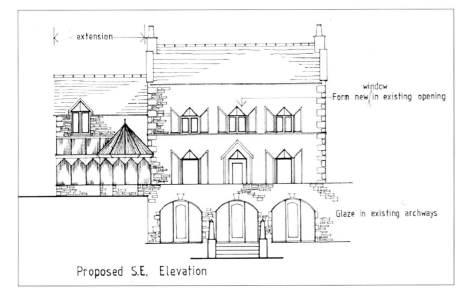

Proposed S.E. Elevation

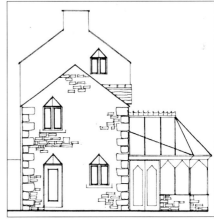

Above: (Left) Oliver's drawing showing the Rock Cottage extension and changes to the archway. (Right) The new extension in profile.

Grown men were in tears telling Sally how much they were owed.

There was one added complication. Glass had been specially cut in the shape required for the new conservatory windows, but had not been delivered. The builder had not paid for it either but, as the Jacksons pointed out, it was not going to be of use to anyone else and so they paid for it themselves..

With the demise of the building contractor, the Jacksons re-hired many of the work-force themselves and, unusually for him, Oliver became a very active project manager. Often Peter would return from work to find Oliver and Sally sharing the problems of the day with the aid of a gin and tonic. The Jacksons appreciated Oliver's contribution immensely and are delighted that their son

Below:
(Left) Rock Cottage's original window shape that Oliver applied to other features.
(Centre) The previous style of bannister and balustrade
(Right) How Oliver applied the window shape to the balustrades.

Andrew, his wife Helen and their family live at Rock Cottage today. "The only criticism you could possibly have had was his costing, which tended to be a bit on the optimistic side", Peter observes with just the slightest hint of understatement.

The Old Chapel

Rock Cottage was not the first Blockley property of note to be redesigned by Oliver Dicks. The first was the old "Ebenezer" Baptist chapel located beyond *The Crown* in the High Street. The Baptist Union sold the chapel, a Grade II listed building, to an American Frank Aliberti in 1987 after obtaining planning permission for residential use in 1986. According to its current owners Nigel and Christine Moor, the property had stood empty since its last Baptist minister left in 1971[4]. The plans submitted by the Baptist Union envisaged reducing the size of the tall arched windows at the front of the building to two panes in height to allow for a new first floor to be positioned beneath them. The three panes below the upper two would be removed and replaced by a rendered wall, beneath which would be constructed new French windows five panes in height with pointed glazing to match the windows above (see illustrations below).

Oliver's plans for the new owner were imaginative and it was obvious that he took considerable pride in them. The eventual outcome reflected something of a collegiate approach by which further design ideas evolved from discussions with Aliberti and his partner Brien Merriman, as well as with other local people involved such as Alan Warburton and Simon Bolton. Another contributor was a Puerto Rican architect Evelio Pina.

According to Simon Bolton's recollection, the only significant design change

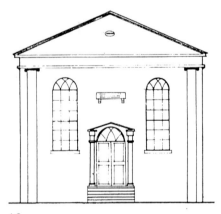 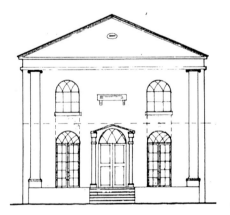 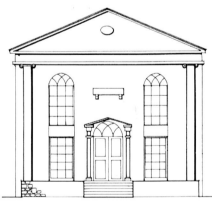

Above:
View from the gates - The Ebenezer Chapel when in active use, with eminent baptist Richard Boswell Belcher standing by his wife's grave.

Below:
The original wrought iron gates at the entrance to the Ebenezer Chapel, since removed and replaced.

introduced by Pina's intervention was to the front windows. Everything else of substance remained as Oliver had designed it. His daughter Kate still remembers the occasions when she would don a hard hat and walk with Oliver through the premises while the building work was being carried out.

Pino's drawings enlarged the height of the top windows from the two panes in the previous plan to four panes, and placed recessed ashlar stone below them. The proposed French windows were changed to conventional single doors with three glazed panels across the width that reflected the original design of the glazing bars. In justification Aliberti told the planners: "My goal is to preserve the austere architectural integrity of the building."

Imagine the conventional interior of a Baptist chapel. On the first floor level at the rear of the building there would have been a gallery of pews across the full width of the chapel, overlooking the main seating area on the ground floor below. A pulpit would stand prominently in front of the congregation, probably with an organ behind although sometimes the organ would be located on the first floor gallery at the other end of the church. Today the interior is very different, as the plans opposite show.

The interior of the building has been stripped completely and replaced by a two-storey residence. Crucially the new design maximises the use of the daylight available from the four existing deep windows - two on each side of the building extending a long way down from the roof. These have to serve both floors of the property, including new rooms that have no external light source of their own. If a conventional first floor had been inserted that reached across the entire building it would have bisected those windows, severely limiting the amount of daylight reaching the ground floor and denying some rooms any daylight at all.

To overcome these challenges, the first floor rooms were located at each end of the building, joined by what the plans describe as a "catwalk" or bridge that allowed light to flood down from the side windows to the ground floor without interruption (see plan). The catwalk design also allowed the original windows to be seen in full from either floor inside.

Two bedrooms with ensuite bathrooms were constructed at one end of the catwalk. At the other end is a large viewing area (shown on the plan as a study) that stretches across almost the full width of the building, accessed by a staircase leading up from the ground floor. Each of the first floor bedrooms were fitted with glazed interior walls that allowed them to "borrow" the daylight from the four side windows beyond. Similarly on the ground floor, the kitchen and adja-

GROUND FLOOR   FIRST FLOOR

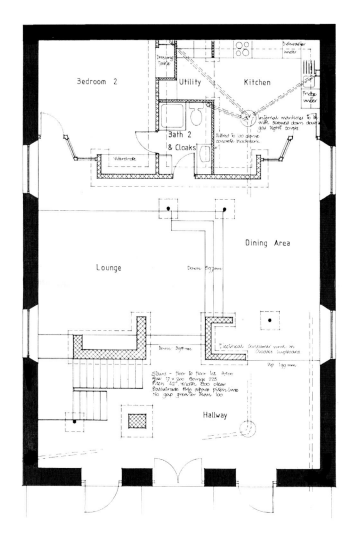
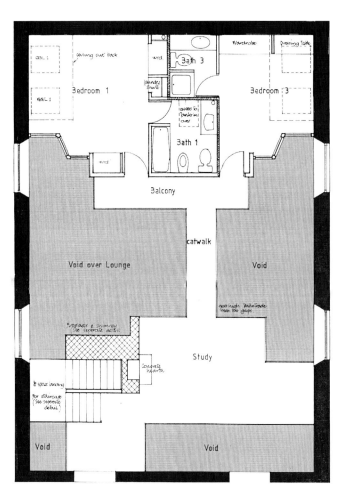

Above:

(Left) Ground floor plan of The Old Chapel believed to have been drawn by Oliver Dicks.   (Right) First floor drawing which was subject to subsequent minor alterations, including reducing the void at the front right so that it no longer extended above the front door. Note the catwalk linking the study to the bedrooms.

Opposite:
Wheelwright House showing the original
wheelwright's premises on the right.

Below:
Oliver's floor plan for the wheelwright's annex
(left), the street profile showing the annex
between Wheelwright House and Halfway
House (centre) and the spiral staircase that was
substituted for the fixed staircase on the initial
plan (right).

cent room (shown as Bedroom 1 on the plan) have glazed walls that fulfil the same function. "The result is a wonderful space", Simon Bolton enthuses. "Ollie had produced the perfect feel for a converted chapel that was admired by numerous local friends at Frank and Brien's parties."

Nigel Moor believes the first (or mezzanine) floor with the catwalk works very well: "It has preserved the full internal height of the chapel and ensured that there is no obstruction to the full length windows on each of the side elevations. There are practical problems such as internal window cleaning and replacing the light bulbs on the light fittings that are suspended the full height from the ceiling of the chapel but these are justified by the design approach."

The entrance to The Old Chapel is through a pair of impressive wrought iron gates beyond which a pathway originally passed between the tombstones of the departed up to the imposing front doors. The original iron gates and pews disappeared in dubious circumstances shortly before the church was sold by the Baptist Union. The current gates are close copies of the originals.[6]

Wheelwright House

A few yards further along the High Street is a relatively small building from which the village wheelwright used to ply his trade. It stands next to, and now forms part of, the property that bears the name Wheelwright House. When Mike and Caroline Howes bought the property, the wheelwright's stone shed was used for storage. By 2002 they were thinking that the shed could be put to better use, whether as an annex to provide extra living accommodation or as an office or even as a self-contained unit to let.

Almost inevitably they were recommended to Oliver Dicks to examine the possibility of converting the building to residential use. The building was redesigned with two storeys - a bedroom, and ensuite shower room on the first floor

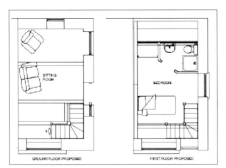  

Opposite page:
*Rear view of Chapel Cottage (bottom right)
viewed from Donkey Lane, with Rock Cottage
in the background*

reached by a spiral staircase from the ground floor. "Oliver used a lot of glass in place of traditional timber balustrades", Caroline recalls. And her memories of Oliver are of someone who was amusing, knowledgeable and helpful: "We worked well together", she says.

Planning consent was obtained without any difficulty and building work took place in 2002. While the work was being carried out, a stone was found bearing the name "José". Caroline Howes is under the impression that the stone dates back to the eighteenth century when a number of the older buildings were erected in High Street. It now forms part of the annex wall.

Chapel Cottage

Heading back along the High Street towards Dovedale, a building protrudes unexpectedly from the main line of properties opposite Rock Cottage. It is called Chapel Cottage but has no connection with the old Baptist Chapel. Originally the property was two buildings - a barn and a cottage - and is rumoured to have been used as a chapel by followers of prophetess Joanna Southcott who lived in Rock Cottage for some years . It is also known to have been used by a local pack of Brownies (the junior branch of the Girlguiding movement) and for guitar lessons. The protruding position of the cottage property suggests that at some stage it formed an island in the High Street with the highway passing along both sides of it. Subsequently one of these two routes must have been closed, allowing more cottages to be built on the land that became available.

Local resident Arthur Tart bought the two buildings in the early nineteen eighties and converted them into a single residence, providing three bedrooms, a bathroom, a sizeable living room, a small kitchen and a garage (see the plan on page 26). The style was fairly basic and typical of the period, with very limited visual appeal.

It was to this dated property that Paul and Julie Dove were to pay a visit in the midst of a rare Blockley blizzard in January 2006. Their plan was to move from the Wirral because Paul had taken on a new job in Leamington Spa.

At first sight Chapel Cottage didn't click as a possible future home: "It was very eighties", Julie recalls. So they returned to their hotel in Chipping Campden for tea. But as professional surveyors they could see potential beyond the initial impression. That evening they returned to *The Crown* in Blockley for a drink, hoping to get a feel for the village as they sat by the log fire. The place was "just buzzing" and the mood was infectious. On the Monday Paul had to return to work and Julie went back to have another look at Chapel Cottage. Three fea-

*Below:
Chapel Cottage as it appears when approached
along the High Street from Dovedale.*

Above:
*The refurbished arched window, previously
concealed by a pelmet and curtains hung from
the lintel that is just visible at the top.*

tures attracted her interest - the 18 foot long oak beams, some "wonderful" oak lintels, and the large arched rear window the impact of which had been obscured by a pelmet and curtains.

Julie came to the conclusion that the cottage "ticked virtually all the boxes". It was fully habitable in its current condition and would therefore enable Paul to move in immediately. It had all the attractions of a period property, without the depressingly dark rooms and low ceilings that sometimes come with them. The rear view was magnificent and the sound of the brook was "really lovely". The small garden was an advantage too. And it was available at an attractive price. The only slight disadvantage was the lack of a "presence" from the street (it faced the opposite direction). They made an offer and the deal was done.

The Doves' nextdoor neighbour in Blockley was to be Tony Drinkwater and they soon met. Not surprisingly they talked about the refurbishment potential. "You need to speak to Ollie Dicks", Tony advised, and soon he was taking Paul for a drink at *The Crown*. "When does Ollie come in?" Paul asked. He didn't need to wait for an answer. Oliver was seated at the bar and immediately introduced himself. Soon they were deep in conversation and Tony left them to it.

Below:
Oliver Dicks' plans showing the interior of Chapel Cottage today and how it looked previously.

Paul and Julie were attracted to the idea of opening up the larger part of the property that had originally been a barn. The front door would lead directly into a large seating area beyond which there would be a kitchen and dining area. From the ground floor the staircase would lead directly to the master bedroom. Paul's thinking was that an open plan would allow the most efficient heating of the building, recognising the probability that energy resources will become increasingly scarce and expensive. The entire area would be heated by electricity, at the core of which would be a range cooker radiating warmth throughout the surrounding area. This would be supplemented by underfloor heating.

The garage area would be converted into additional living accommodation with a bedroom and bathroom upstairs.

Not everything met with Oliver Dicks' approval. Indeed he was really unhappy about the lack of walls upstairs, giving open access to the master bedroom. "It will ruin the house and you will regret it", he exclaimed grumpily. But when it came to developing the Doves' ideas into viable plans, he reverted to his "can do" attitude. As Paul puts it: "He blended discipline with an ear to what you wanted. And he could be great fun."

One of Oliver's pet ideas was to include an American style fridge freezer in the kitchen. He would sit at his computer screen, juggling with room shapes and sizes. "Yes we can do that", he would insist, despite the Doves' scepticism. It was an idea that never came to pass.

There were other ideas too that were eventually discarded. One was to design banquette seating for the dining room that would provide storage space inside. The idea was a good one, although some of the styles that Oliver accessed from his computer library were rather wild. In the end the idea was deferred - for the time being at least.

Another brainwave came when the redundant fireplace was removed from the corner of the living room. It provided an ideal opportunity to insert a rooflight where the chimney had been in the new ensuite bathroom.

Paul moved into Chapel Cottage on his own before any work began. He would often receive a phone call at work when Oliver was wanting to discuss an aspect of the plans with him. So they would meet up in the evening and discuss the matter more extensively over a pint. The relationship flourished and before long Oliver was inviting Paul to his home where he would cook him a meal. "Fried corn beef hash was his *piece de resistance*", Paul recalls, and it was always preceded by a glass of Plymouth gin. On one occasion Oliver responded to Paul's love of asparagus by driving off to Evesham to get some.

Above:
Chapel Cottage from the rear showing the arched window (bottom right) after refurbishment.

27

Choosing the colour of paint for the exterior walls became a major public event. Julie tells how they had obtained various paint samples from the local builders' merchants Travis Perkins and were innocuously exploring their suitability on the wall alongside the High Street: "Suddenly everybody appeared and they each had their own ideas." Oliver had his own very firm ideas too: "If you don't use this colour, he said, citing his preferred choice, "the planners won't approve." It wasn't the first occasion Oliver had called on the planners in aid of his personal preference! Then a local interior designer Alison Hunt came along the street. "It needs to be Farrow & Ball 'Bone'", she suggested. And that was the colour the Doves settled on without even obtaining a tester pot. Oliver disapproved, and showed it.

The building work was completed in six months and the Doves moved back in on 1 July 2008. Like everyone else, they faced the inevitable challenge of finding a way to reward Oliver for his help. "We don't worry about that sort of thing here", Oliver explained. "We just help each other out in this village."

A firm friendship evolved between the two families and, with the project complete, Oliver and Jean joined Paul and Julie for supper in October 2008. They were not to know that it would be their last meal together although Oliver had been undergoing treatment and brought a supply of oxygen with him. Everyone was in positive mood. Part of the purpose of the evening was to plan a trip together on the Norfolk Broads. Oliver was eating well and in good humour. When the dessert came, it was apple crumble. But where was the custard? In Oliver's view crumble wasn't crumble without custard. All Julie could offer as an alternative was ice cream. True to character, Oliver accepted that alternative but demanded a heated knife with which to cut it.

Malvern House

A visitor to Blockley would be a little confused and surprised to learn that it was the first home of Malvern House girls' boarding school late in the nineteenth century[5]. Admittedly, it wasn't home for long. In 1897 the school moved to Malvern and subsequently became part of the Abbey School which in turn is now part of Malvern St James's independent school[6]. However, illustrated on page 30 is a prize-winner's copy of Sir Edward Creasy's book *The Fifteen Decisive Battles of the World: Marathon to Waterloo* that was presented in 1896 with the school's name and Blockley location stamped in gilt on the cover[7].

It is just possible to picture this tall four storey building housing about 14 boarders and staff, but today it is home to a much smaller family - Alistair and

Opposite page:
Front view of Malvern House. Blockley Brook flows behind.
Below:
Malvern House in former times

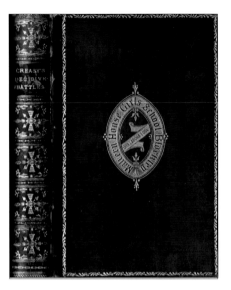

Above: The stamp of Malvern House Girls School in Blockley on the cover of a prize book presented by Florence & Margaret Judson to pupil Grace Begbie in 1896. Below: The inscription.

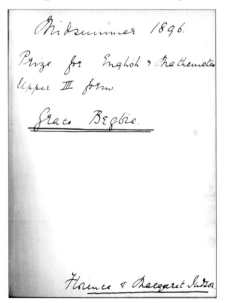

Lesley Campbell and (occasionally) their grown-up children. Prior to that it had been converted into flats by the local property developer Harold da Silva and subsequently acquired by Sue and Dominic Rossi who occupied the top two floors and let the rest.

Al Campbell was walking towards *The Crown* one evening early in 1996 when he met Dominic Rossi emerging from his driveway. It transpired that Dominic was planning to sell the property and, knowing of Al's passing interest in the building, he offered him first refusal. Leaving aside its structural condition, Malvern House had a number of attractions. Built alongside Malvern Mill in the High Street, it was positioned within a few metres of Blockley Brook. It came with an acre of land. It had plenty of parking space (a rare amenity in Blockley). And it provided a home that Al and his new partner Les could create together.

"It was in a bad state", Al recalls, but Les puts it more bluntly: "It was awful. I had never seen anything like it!" Her mother said they must be mad. Nevertheless completion of the purchase went ahead while Al and Les were relaxing by a swimming pool in Lanzarote.

The Rossis had been planning some alterations to the property and Oliver Dicks had already done some drawings for a garage and some replacement windows. So it was not long before Al was meeting up with Oliver at *The Great Western Arms* to discuss his own ideas.

Almost immediately Oliver volunteered to look round the property. But four years were to elapse before approval was eventually obtained for the extensive alterations and restoration they planned together.

Priority was given to the garage as planning consent had already been obtained and was likely to expire fairly soon. Here a drama was about to unfold. As the builders dug out the soil for the foundations, they discovered blue clay and then a spring in the corner of the site. Al tells the story like this: "The local authority building controller said we should call in a structural engineer. And the structural engineer said we should obtain a geological survey. We had to redesign the garage with the primary function of providing a retaining wall to hold back the hillside and a secondary function as a garage."

The cavity wall had to be half a metre thick with a double density inner wall and the cavity filled with reinforced concrete. Not content with that, the overall dimensions had to be extended so that there would be room inside for a third wall to be constructed if the proposed cavity wall was not strong enough to hold back the hillside.

Apart from the geological challenge, there was much debate about what to put on top of the garage roof. Oliver suggested a clock. Only when it had been completed did it become obvious that the clock's hands could not be altered from ground level. One day, when Al was feeling particularly irritated that the clock was telling the wrong time, he resolved to find a way to reach it. It seemed less high from the hillside behind so he scrambled up to the rear. Manouvring himself around the clock tower, he eventually succeeded in turning the hands. A triumph! When Les returned from work, Al could not conceal his pride. "But why did you do it today?" Les enquired. "The clocks are due to be changed by an hour tonight!"

Attention then turned to the house itself. "The primary aim was to put the whole house back to how it was originally", Al explains. "But to do so we had to wear down a succession of listed building officers in the planning department."

Externally it was the rear of the property that was most in need of restoration. The windows were scattered about in random positions and were entirely out of keeping with the character and period of the building (see drawing). The planners had previously approved a modest modification sought by the Rossis, but it had been no more than a partial tidying up.

There were two main components of the Campbells' plan. First they wanted to recreate a symmetrical arrangement of windows more in keeping with the property's origins. In particular they wanted to replace two windows that were positioned above one another at the centre of the back wall by a single deep one that would let more light into the interior stairwell, while restoring some historic character to the outside appearance. Secondly - and more boldly - they wanted to build balconies outside the two replacement first floor French windows.

Below left: Malvern House from the rear prior to its renovation. Below right: The redesigned rear elevation as drawn by Oliver Dicks with renewed symmetry plus two balconies.

In their dealings with the planners Al and Les found a helpful ally in their neighbour Jeremy Bourne who lives at Malvern Mill. To their surprise and delight Jeremy remembered from his childhood that there had been a deep window at the rear before. He was also very much in favour of the restoration of the property generally and was able to write a letter of support.

The bigger challenges related to the balconies. Al wanted them. Oliver didn't. Oliver feared the planners would not approve such a feature and their initial reactions reinforced those fears. The balconies would not "be in keeping", they said. "In keeping with what?" Al enquired, noting that another neighbouring property Spindlebrook had a balcony and that Orchard Bank had balconies too. Eventually the planners conceded.

As will have become evident already, arguing with Oliver was an every day occurrence for those whose company he kept. As Al puts it: "If he had an opinion you would know about it, and I never knew him not to have an opinion. He was always right unless you could eloquently prove him wrong." Offer an opinion of your own and the retort would often come back: "You're wrong". Les describes it as probably Oliver's most common phrase.

But although he always had his own opinions he would also respect those of his clients and investigate their ideas thoroughly. Then he would often add extra value to the idea, saying: "If you do it like this, it would be even better!"

Oliver's advice could often be invaluable. For example, there was the day when an unknown villager made a complaint to the planning department resulting in the sudden arrival of an enforcement officer who insisted all work should stop pending a visit from the planning officer the following morning. Sensing Al would not be overly welcoming to any planning officer in such circumstances, Oliver's advice was that it would be best if he was somewhere else that day.

Internally, there were lots of discoveries while stripping the building back to its original structure. During work to restore the area that is now the dining room a cupboard was found set into the outside wall. It was lined with newspapers from the nineteen twenties. More serious was the discovery that many of the main supporting beams had rotted and needed to be replaced.

Fitting out the interior also became a major project. Shawn Deacon made a big contribution to the design of many of the rooms although Oliver designed the kitchen: "I liked it as soon as I saw it", Les recalls.

While work proceeded it would not be unusual for Oliver to have let himself into the house and settled down with a newspaper as he waited for Al or Les to appear. Like everyone else, they discovered very early in their working relation-

ship that Oliver wouldn't take any money for his efforts. "It was 'his' village",
Les explains. "He knew the place inside out and enjoyed doing the work."

Box Cottage

Those who have studied the history of Blockley will be aware that its early
trading roots were at the Dovedale (south western) end. Commercial traders
and others would approach the village by way of Donkey Lane - now little more
than a track that leads off the B4479 road as it descends towards the village
from Bourton on the Hill.

That track narrows to no more than a footpath as it branches away from
Brook Lane and leads on to Dovedale itself. But in its heyday, donkey carts
would carry their loads along this route and offload and store their boxes of
wares in a barn at the end of the lane. More recently that barn and two adjacent
cottages have been combined to form Box Cottage. Behind Box Cottage other
buildings on the banks of the brook originally housed the village tannery and a
washhouse.

Box Cottage and the buildings behind were bought by Patricia Milligan-
Baldwin in 2001. The premises were in serious need of updating and the new
owners wanted a study, more storage and better living accommodation. Much
could be achieved if the disused attic could be put to better use.

Patricia was known first and foremost as a judge who, like many other pro-
fessionals with jobs elsewhere, viewed Blockley as a place of rest and retreat.
But there was much more to her talents than legal prowess. She had trained
originally as an architect and planner at Liverpool University. Then she went on
to study city planning at London University. Now Blockley offered her an opportunity to give new expression to her property-related knowledge. And in
Oliver Dicks she found the perfect sparring partner with whom to debate and

Below:
Front view of Box Cottage and adjacent
properties before inclusion of dormer windows.

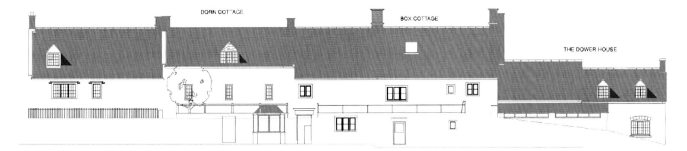

Opposite page:
Box Cottage today, flanked by Dorn Cottage
(left) and the Dower House (right) at the
Dovedale end of the High Street.

Below:
Oliver Dicks' drawings of how the front and
rear elevations might look with dormer windows
(only two were included at the front eventually).

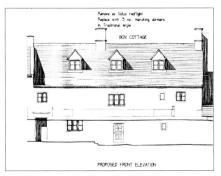

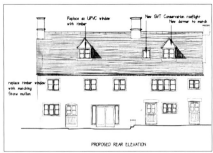

develop ideas.

They first met as neighbours and it soon became clear that it would be useful for her to run her ideas past Oliver before tackling Cotswold District Council on planning matters.

So they set to work. The lawyer would put her case with all the knowledge and advocacy skills she could muster. The planner would counter with all the reasons why the Council would throw it out. They would debate the merits of the case with fervour and mutual respect - not so much as client and professional adviser but as knowledgable equals. And soon a glass of claret would emerge to accompany the proceedings. Patricia puts it like this: "He was a good listener. He wouldn't block an idea and, if persuaded, he would be emboldened to pursue it. He had a genuine love of the architectural landscape of the village. It was a delight to debate with him. A real treat. I learned a lot from him."

Oliver doubted whether the planners would approve the addition of two dormer windows at the front of the property. His reservations were so strong that they provoked Patricia to tour the village and study typical dormer motifs on other properties. She returned with such convincing evidence that Oliver was persuaded to include them in his plans.

But, when Patricia proposed introducing dormers at the rear, Oliver remained doggedly sceptical. "I'll draw it", he said with all the enthusiasm of a dead sheep, "but you are in for a long fight!" True to his word the plans were submitted and several weeks later Patricia set off to Canada to visit her family. Arriving at Vancouver airport, she sent an email to Oliver enquiring about progress. Back came the reply: "You bugger, you got it all!" And all within eight weeks.

Another of Patricia's ideas that tested Oliver's equilibrium was a desire to wind an internal staircase around the original chimney. "If you do that, the front wall is going to fall down", Oliver retorted in his typically gruff voice. But between them they found a technically sound solution and in Patricia's view no-one would believe it had not always been there.

Patricia sees planning as a power play. It's about problem solving and inveigling approval. Experience had taught Oliver not to show any malice in his dealings with planners. He knew the planning process intimately and would never knowingly be party to anything he knew would be a resounding failure.

His willingness to share his knowledge helped Patricia develop sound planning arguments. "He was hugely generous with his time. His love of buildings was a real reason for him to get up in the morning. And his work constantly honed his expertise, giving him a special place in the Blockley community."

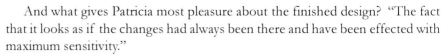

Top:
Rear view of The Old Bakery before alteration.
Above:
The Old Bakery after Oliver's addition of the
conservatory.
Opposite page:
The Old Bakery viewed from the High Street

And what gives Patricia most pleasure about the finished design? "The fact that it looks as if the changes had always been there and have been effected with maximum sensitivity."

The Old Bakery

At the junction of the High Street with School Lane is a row of properties that over time have been merged into one to become known as The Old Bakery. The property is located within the conservation area although not listed. As its name implies, for many years the building housed the village bakery, but it has also accommodated a fire station (it is still possible to see where the fire bell hung), a ladies' hairdresser and - it is believed - even a doctor's surgery.

More recently the premises became an award-winning guest house where Linda Helme offered top quality accommodation and dining. But in 2005, after the unexpected death of her partner, she decided to sell up and move. The buyers were Tim and Chris Boddington who were looking for a place to which they could retire from their Hertfordshire home.

"We came here thinking we would do nothing", Tim recalls. But living in the house caused them to think again. The sitting room began to feel rather small, especially when they were visited by their ever-increasing family. And the kitchen was rather dark. So they contemplated an extension to the existing sitting room and the introduction of two windows looking out from the kitchen towards School Lane. "We can do this quite cheaply", thought Tim and Chris. In the words of Alexander Pope: hope springs eternal…

They were introduced to Oliver Dicks by their neighbours Rob and Carol Willott who lived opposite at The Old Royal Oak. According to Tim, Oliver was "round like a shot". The brief was simple: open up the sitting room towards the garden and let in more light. Hours were spent in Oliver's office, enthralled by his computer wizardry as he moved lines and objects around the screen: "Drawings were done within minutes - he was so enthusiastic", Chris recollects.

Right:
Oliver Dicks' drawings for the additional windows in the southwest wall of The Old Bakery and for the new conservatory at the rear of the building.

Two new windows
SW ELEVATION

SE ELEVATION

Above:

The sitting room fireplace in The Old Bakery before the builders applied a sledge hammer to it (left) and the original fireplace rediscovered (right).

Opposite page:

Side view of Lower Farmhouse as it looks today.

Below:

Front elevation of the original farmhouse before any alterations were made.

"He was a very good listener. You could almost see the cogs of his brain turning. And he was good at accommodating other peoples' ideas."

The extension to the living room was designed as a conservatory and so the work was not subject to building regulation inspection in addition to planning permission. Oliver's initial thinking was to create what is called a "lantern roof" sloping down from the centre, similar to the one he had designed for The Manor House[8]. The aim was to enable the sloping glass roof to start from as close to the existing house wall as possible and maximise the amount of light flowing into the sitting room. To achieve this, it was necessary to raise the position of the existing upstairs window sill.

Tim says it took Oliver quite a lot of time to persuade them that the external appearance of the extension would not look too grand for its surroundings: "He showed us various alternatives and eventually was proved to be absolutely right in his choice."

Building work began in May 2006 The footings were dug out by hand under a boiling sun. Then, as the work progressed, builder Phil Dunn looked at the existing fireplace in the sitting room and came to the conclusion that it was probably false. Returning a little later with a sledge hammer, his suspicions were proved right. Not only was the existing fireplace concealing a second one. That second one also concealed a third! The discovery enabled the Boddingtons to restore the original fireplace and gain about a metre of extra room space.

Lower Farmhouse

Plenty of landmarks announce to visitors that they have arrived in Blockley when approaching by road from Bourton on the Hill. Not least is the sharp bend as the road navigates its way past Lower Brook House. The bend is made all the more hazardous by the emergence of Pasture Lane from the right and the entrance to what used to be Lower Farm on the left.

The last tenants of Lower Farm were Martin and Joan Dee who moved further south to Park Farm in about 1979. The disused farmhouse and outbuildings were then bought by Rob and Gill Greenstock. They converted the outbuildings into holiday homes and refurbished the old farmhouse for themselves. Later they sold the entire site to the Prowting building firm which then rented out the holiday homes and allocated the farmhouse to a site manager. In 2006 Prowting decided to sell off each property on the site as an individual unit, including the farmhouse itself as a self-contained property. The cottages ceased to have access to Lower Street but instead used a rear entrance off School Lane.

Above: Lower Farmhouse in the days when it was a working farm before the Greenstocks bought it

Below:
Oliver's drawing of the east elevation as seen from Lower Street, showing dining room extension (nearest) and the two-storey extension to the left.

EAST ELEVATION

The timing of the sell-off coincided with a search by Henry and Sam Goodrick-Clarke for a family home in the area. Henry's mother and father - Celia and Andrew - were already Blockley residents who by coincidence lived at the Old Silk Mill which had once been home to Oliver's parents[9].

As they looked around the farmhouse and its surroundings, Henry and Sam discovered it had more to offer than could have been imagined if viewed only from the road. Built with three storeys and occupying a relatively small piece of land, the house looked deceptively small. In fact it had five bedrooms some of which had been added in Victorian times when the original 200 year old building was extended. A number of the timbers contain old mortice joints that show signs of having been used elsewhere and Henry speculates that they were removed from disused mills and similar buildings.

Not much had been done to the property after the Greenstocks had left it. That was not without some benefit, however, as the Greenstocks had installed a very good Aga kitchen range before leaving. Nevertheless parts of the property needed to be brought up to date to reflect 21st century styles of family accommodation.

The farmhouse formed only part of the property being sold. It also included the land alongside the Blockley brook as it runs below the Manor House, as well as what used to be a common parking area alongside a number of garages. Henry and Sam could see the attraction of the grounds - "it was perfect for children" says Sam - and the farmhouse itself was a nice property that offered great potential as a family home. So they decided they would try to buy it.

The sale of the farmhouse was by sealed bids and, having been disappointed once before, Henry and Sam tried to prepare themselves for disappointment again. Imagine their delight when their bid was successful. All that was then required was a designer and a builder, and neither were hard to find. Henry Goodrick-Clarke was a builder himself and he knew Oliver Dicks very well both through the family connection and as a drinking companion with his father on occasional Sunday nights at *The Crown*.

The structural changes involved creating a larger open plan kitchen and living area in keeping with modern practice, adding an ensuite bathroom to the master bedroom above, building a new dining room accessed from the kitchen, and linking the main house to an outbuilding that would be converted into a cloakroom and an office for Henry's business (shown as " utility" on the plan).

When Henry shared the good news of the property purchase and their ambitions for its upgrading with Oliver, his response was immediate: "Don't worry.

Ground floor **First floor** **Second floor**

Left:
Floor plan showing how Oliver designed the
extension of Lower Farmhouse. The original
property outline is shown in black with
Victorian addition outline in grey.

I'll sort that out for you." Being fairly busy at the time, Oliver showed Henry how to measure up the property . Once done Henry sat down one evening with Oliver, Oliver's computer and two or three extremely strong gin and tonics. "It was virtually all done in that evening", Henry recalls.

The main challenge was to drop the floor level of the new dining room below that of the rest of the house in order to allow its roof line to drop down too. Sam recalls the thinking: "He was very conscious of Blockley elevations and knew that's what the planners would like."

With the drawings completed, Oliver phoned Henry to ask for a cheque to take with him to the planners. Five weeks later, full planning consent had been obtained. As a full-time builder, Henry could only devote his spare time to the family home and it took him two years to complete the project. But his praise for Oliver's contribution is unstinting: "He was always willing to stand up to planners and those responsible for building control. He was down to earth and would always help you out, being over-generous with his time." His training as a surveyor rather than an architect was a bonus as far as Henry was concerned: "You knew that everything Ollie produced could be built."

Henry admits that he would not have wanted to engage in arguments with building control officers, but Oliver was prepared to do so. His readiness to argue reflected a temperament that would not have sat comfortably with the role of a typical project manager, a role that Oliver would normally avoid. As Henry puts it: "He had such strong views that some clients would not like it."

CHAPTER 4

The Mills and The Manor

*"Ollie's strength was that he knew exactly what property
owners could get away with. We were really thrilled. He did
a sterling job."*

The Old Silk Mill[10] is perhaps the most renowned of Blockley's mills. Before it became home to Oliver Dicks' parents[11] it had featured in the film *Rip van Winkle*. Later US army tanks were parked on its lawn in preparation for the D-Day landings. So it is hardly surprising that Oliver continued to take an interest after the property was purchased by Andrew and Celia Goodrick-Clarke in 1987[12].

In design terms Oliver's contribution was relatively modest as the major up-grading of the property had been assigned to an Oxford firm of architects. Nevertheless the hand of Dicks can be seen in the outcome.

For example, the architects designed a stand-alone garage to be erected in the grounds, but the Goodrick-Clarkes were uncomfortable with its appearance. According to Andrew it looked more like an engine shed: "It was too simple - with not enough Cotswold character". He related his concerns to Oliver and asked him to take a look.

When Oliver arrived, somewhat to Andrew's surprise he started examining the footings being dug for the garage. Without any hesitation he assailed the builder: "Tell your digger driver he's using the wrong size bucket." In Oliver's expert view the footings had to be wider and deeper.

Turning his attention to the garage design, Oliver suggested that a classic Cotswold "label moulding" should be inserted above the garage doors to match the mouldings that could be seen above the windows and doors of the mill itself. Oliver's advice was accepted and it achieved the desired effect.

"Oliver was always interested in what we were doing and said he liked what we did", Andrew recalls.

Celia tells of the occasion when they decided to move an internal wall by

*Opposite page:
The front of The Old Silk Mill (left) showing the new garage (right) for which Oliver contributed advice.
Below:
Oliver Dicks checks the depth of the footings for the new garage at The Old Silk Mill (formerly Sleepy Hollow).*

Above (left to right): Henry Goodrick-Clarke (centre of picture) helps install the new sluice gate designed by Oliver Dicks; The classic mouldings above the windows of The Old Silk Mill (centre) that Oliver recommended be replicated on the front of the new garage; The garage under construction incorporating the moulding suggested by Oliver Dicks (right).

Opposite page:
Northwick Mill after alteration. The new extension can be seen on the right.
Below:
Northwick Mill before refurbishment. (The mill race is situated to the left of the building.)

about two feet so as to give better access to the French doors. In doing so some veneered plywood panelling had to be removed, only to reveal genuine oak panelling that Oliver's parents had covered up.

In 1995 the wooden sluice gate at the lower end of the mill pond was found to have broken into bits and was no longer fit for purpose. Having related the situation to Oliver in *The Crown* , Andrew was soon in receipt of drawings for a steel replacement. It was installed by Neil Johnson, a local builder who was uncle to Andrew's son Henry. Henry also helped with the installation.

Northwick Mill

Of all the 13 mills that once fuelled Blockley's local industry, Northwick Mill is furthest downstream. It is also nearest to Northwick Park - home to the benevolent land-owning Spencer Churchill family until 1964. Among its other distinguishing features is the fact that it was the last of the former mills to retain its mill race and wheel. Sadly, that is all that now remains of the original workings.

Originally the mill and surrounding farmland all formed part of the Northwick Estate. The last tenant farmer was Jack Turvey who managed the mill until it ceased to be viable in about 1938. Thereafter the Turvey family continued to live there and farm the land, buying it from the Estate in about 1979. After Jack Turvey died the mill and much of the surrounding land was bought by Michael Smith who lives at the adjacent Northwick Mill Farm. He discovered that the oak axle of the mill wheel had rotted and restored it to its former condition.

Johnty Stoker bought the property from Michael Smith in 1995 to make a home for himself, his new wife Sharan and their two dogs. It was modest in size

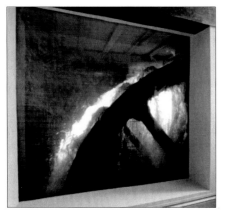

Above: The only remaining water wheel in Blockley as seen from the dining room of Northwick Mill.

although located in a beautiful setting. The space limitations became apparent immediately upon entering the ground floor where a single room accommodated both the kitchen and the dining area. Having settled in, Johnty and Sharan invited their neighbours to lunch. The conversation and drink began to flow and in due course their guests suggested adding a new kitchen to the end of the building.

Warming to the idea, the next move was to follow in the footsteps of many other Blockley property owners and meet up with Oliver Dicks. Sharan's father was a surveyor and could probably have done a perfectly good job for them, so why go to Oliver? "In Blockley, that's where you went", explains Sharan in a slightly incredulous tone of voice: "If you wanted something done, Ollie did it!"

Oliver's idea was not just to build a new kitchen but also to create a first floor link through from the existing study onto a balcony from which all the culinary activity below could be surveyed. "It sailed through the Council planning department", Sharan recalls. "Ollie's strength was that he knew exactly what property owners could get away with. We were really thrilled. He did a sterling job." They were particularly pleased about the way in which Oliver was able to make the extension fit so sympathetically with the existing mill.

On Sharan's own admission, Oliver's only problem was managing her expectations. While she would be anxious about every possible problem that might beset the planning process, Oliver was laid back and calm. His advice to her was simple and to the point: "Be a good girl and do as you're told." His voice would be firm, but almost always followed by a short chuckle.

The construction work began in July 2001 and it was not long before the first complication arose. In preparing the footings, the builders disturbed drainage pipework serving the mill and three adjacent properties which was found to have been laid directly below the site of the new kitchen extension. "We had to restore all the pipework", Sharan recalls. "It cost a lot for no visible benefit."

Then there was a slight hiccup in the sourcing of timber for the new balcony.

Below:
Oliver Dicks' floor plan for Northwick Mill showing kitchen extension on the right.

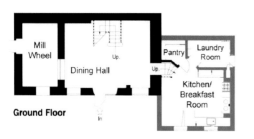

Ground Floor

First Floor

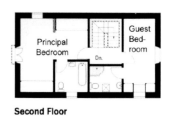

Second Floor

Above:
The kitchen extension to Northwick Mill under construction (left); The new first floor balcony overlooking the kitchen (centre); The first floor balcony as seen from the kitchen below (right).

Oliver had specified oak. And although Johnty owns one of the biggest timber merchants in the UK, to his embarrassment he could not obtain any. Predictably Oliver knew somewhere else to look and they managed to obtain enough of the required oak from a sawmill near Snowshill.

One of the most interesting features of the old mill is the wheel itself over which water still pours. It can be seen from the ground floor dining room through a glass panel and the Stokers thought about opening it up a little more. But Oliver counselled against doing anything with the glass on the grounds that, if it doesn't leak, it is best left alone.

Oliver could be relied upon to point out any potential stupidity: "Dear boy, at times you really can be very stupid", he would say. But Johnty loved and respected his candour: "Such honesty from another could offend, but never from Ollie."

Predictably the work took longer than expected and the new kitchen did not become operational until the following Easter. But Johnty and Sharan had no serious regrets - apart from being unable to find a way to pay for Oliver's help.

Saw & Bone Mill

A short distance upstream from Northwick Mill is the site of the disused Saw & Bone Mill that once formed part of the Northwick Estate. As its name implies, the mill had been used to saw timber and create bone meal for use on the estate. At one stage the building also housed the Estate Office from where Captain Spencer-Churchill's bailiff Conrad Warner exercised considerable influence. In scale it was perhaps not the biggest mill in Blockley, but it provided an ideal location for a residence - overlooking a small mill pond and passing brook. And that is what attracted Alan Savery to buy it in 1976.

However, the selling agents were only prepared to sell the entire 2.5 acre site

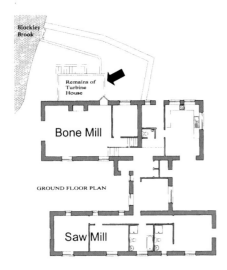

Above: The Saw & Bone Mill after refurbishment as a house by Alan Savery, with disused turbine house arrowed.

Opposite page:
The Saw & Bone Mill in the winter sun today with part of the mill pond in the foreground.
Below:
Proposed Garden Room extension to right of Saw & Bone Mill above previous turbine house

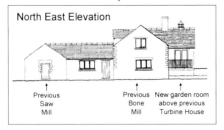

which included six cottages- some of them derelict - and the mill pond itself. The site also had become the dumping ground for all sorts of rubble and unwanted possessions, abandoned vehicles, old gates and even the partial remains of an army truck.

Alan Savery is a public health engineer by profession whose career evolved into the public sector where he progressed to the position of Director of Environmental Heath and Housing at Stratford on Avon. His training had also embraced building surveying and he was an enthusiastic property developer. So the opportunity to refurbish the six cottages adjacent to the Saw & Bone Mill for letting to holiday makers was too good to miss. And then there was the derelict mill itself…

The current building dates from 1837 when it was constructed with a conventional water wheel to drive the machinery. In 1927 the wheel was replaced by a turbine which had fallen into disrepair by the time Alan acquired the property. Having restored the adjacent cottages he set about restoring the mill premises themselves and converting them to a home for his family. In 1983 he had started flirting with the idea of doing something with the remains of the disused turbine house and utilising its water power.

A trend was emerging towards energy conservation and the pursuit of renewable energy sources. Initially the capital cost of re-establishing a water mill as an energy source was not economically justifiable. But circumstances change and more recently Alan concluded that the situation had reversed. In his view the mill was probably the best place in the village to capture existing water energy resources. "If I can't make it work economically, no-one can", he mused.

So he devised a plan to reinstate the water wheel - currently expected to be completed in 2010 - and to build an extension to the original mill premises above it. Alan set about doing some preliminary sketches and handed them to Oliver Dicks to refine on his computer for submission to the council planning department. "He was very good at computer aided design", Alan says.

Alan first met Oliver through an introduction by mutual friends. They became occasional drinking mates while Alan was refurbishing the cottages and the mill. Such was Alan's dedication to property development at the time that on one occasion it prompted Oliver to remark: "You should get out more." They decided to take up bowling together and joined the Northwick Bowling Club. The level of their commitment to the sport may be evidenced by the fact that they bought only one set of bowls between them.

"He had universal appeal", Alan recalls, "with no airs or graces. A very

Opposite page:
The Manor House from the south, showing the new Orangery on the right.

Below:
Oliver's drawing of the en-suite bathroom to replace the abandoned sewing room, including instructions about stabilising the wobbly partition.
Bottom:
The old sewing room before conversion to an en-suite bathroom for the bedroom beyond; to the right is the unstable partition.

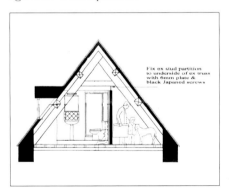

sociable man. A character. A bon viveur. I love the whole building thing, but Oliver loved it even more."

The Manor House

By far the most prominent and beautiful residence in Blockley is the Manor House. Sited immediately south-east of the parish church, it forms a prominent landmark to anyone approaching the village from Bourton on the Hill. In its early days the Manor House provided a summer palace for the Bishops of Worcester and a stop-over for them and their entourage when travelling to London. In the early 15th century the house fell into disrepair. Then it was leased to the Palmer family who razed it to the ground in the middle of the 16th century and rebuilt it much in the style of the present property.

In 1995 it was bought by George and Zöe Thompson who restored it from a crumbling ruin to the comfortable family home it is today. Oliver had no association with that project, but he quickly formed an association with its owners. Whenever they visited Blockley the Thompsons would partake of some lunchtime refreshment at *The Great Western Arms*. "Every time I went in there, he was there", George recalls. "That's when I first met him and how we became friends."

Not long after George and Zöe had moved into their refurbished home, they turned their attention to making better use of an outbuilding that had once been the gardener's cottage. The lower floor offered excellent storage space, but the top floor - which was on the same level as the ground floor of the Manor House itself - was begging for another use. Zöe liked the idea of a swimming pool. Oliver favoured a snooker room - perhaps because he was good at snooker - and George lent his gentle weight towards snooker too. So a snooker room it would be. Oliver designed the conversion which involved creating an additional A-frame to support the ceiling and match an existing one, as well as reinforcing the floor to accommodate the weight of the slate slabs that provide the base of the snooker table. "They did a very good job", Zöe acknowledges, even if it didn't provide her with the swimming pool she had hoped for.

A year or two later Zöe's attention was drawn to an old sewing room on the top floor. In the distant past it had been used to make garments using silk manufactured in the village mills. There were still a few silk pins littered around to prove it. More surprisingly the room also was home to a motley collection of old tyres and wheels.

In the next room the Thompsons had created a double bedroom and they

Photograph: Tony Skellett

Above: The rear of the "crumbling wreck" of the Manor House as the Thompsons found it when they purchased the property in 1995, showing where the orangery is now located.

thought the old sewing room would make an ideal ensuite shower room. However, there was one big obstacle: an unstable seven feet high partition separated the sewing room from the corridor leading to the bedroom. So Oliver was called in to advise on stabilising the wobbly partition and to design the shower room.

But Oliver's biggest assignment at the Manor House was the construction of the orangery. The plan was to build it on to the south-eastern wall adjacent to the lounge and kitchen, benefitting from the sunshine it would enjoy (weather permitting) throughout the day.

The first question asked by the planners was: why do you think that an orangery would be an appropriate addition? In response the Thompsons explained that orangeries were very much in fashion at the time the Manor House was built. Zöe had a picture in her mind of how the orangery should look and Oliver applied his considerable skills to reflect her thinking in his plans. The result was a Georgian style structure in keeping with the 18th century - the period when the adjacent and most recent part of the Manor House had been built.

Eager to minimise any possible planning objections, Oliver's design allowed the orangery to be "removable" so that it could never be seen as structurally reliant on the existing building. This was particularly important because the Manor House had been constructed without the benefit of modern concrete footings. To achieve the desired structural independence a pillar would be erected in the corner near the house and set in 10 feet of concrete. This would support steel

Below left: Oliver's drawing of the floor plan for the Manor House orangery. Below right: Oliver's drawing showing the south elevation of the Manor House with the orangery on the right as it appears today.

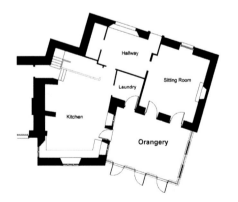

SOUTH ELEVATION

joists reaching to the new outer walls which in turn would support the orangery roof.

The work started with the digging of footings going down eight feet. But this could only proceed if a geological expert was present throughout in case any valuable archeological treasure might be exposed. Sadly no such treasure was found.

One of the challenges faced during construction was the need to match new Cotswold stone with old, and to re-cut it where necessary. Zöe thinks they did an excellent job and George says the new stone looked old from the beginning because of the fossils that were within it. The match was helped by the fact that the builders scrubbed clean every existing stone as well.

And what is their assessment, now that the work has been finished?

"We eat, drink, read and live in here", says George, "and it looks as if it has always been here."

"It's so comfortable too", adds Zöe. "It provides a versatile playroom for our grandchildren. We needn't have the rest of the house! It's so important that it's become our living room. And when you move into the adjacent sitting room with its deep upholstery - so cosy and warm - it's a perfect complement to the orangery."

The sitting room may well be very warm but it can never have been as hot as some of the debates George would have with Oliver at *The Great Western Arms*. Both being argumentative characters, they would often be in the bar late in the evening and finish up in a heated argument - usually on a sporting matter. Early the following evening George would return to the pub for a quick drink and remark to the landlord John Ferguson: "Wasn't Ollie argumentative last night!" Then after George had gone home, Oliver would arrive, sit himself on his customary stool and say: "Wasn't George argumentative last night!"

CHAPTER 5

Houses of Character

"He was not like the typical architect I had been used to. He was receptive and creative, and he knew what would satisfy the planners."

Opposite page:
Garden Cottage as it appears today viewed from Blockley Brook.
Below:
The same view of Garden Cottage before the alterations were carried out by Dick and Lisa Robinson.

Almost opposite Rock Cottage towards the Dovedale end of the High Street stands a house that once enjoyed not only a very large garden but also a gardener's cottage to go with it. Subsequently the site has been split into two plots. One of them comprises the original gardener's cottage - unsurprisingly called Garden Cottage - with the garden sloping gently down to the brook below.

Dick and Lisa Robinson bought Garden Cottage in 2001. They had been looking for a bolt-hole from their Cambridgeshire home to which they might eventually retire.

Garden Cottage was not the only property the Robinsons looked at in Blockley. By a strange coincidence their attention had been drawn first to a property in Northwick Terrace which at the time was being sold by none other than Oliver Dicks[13]. But Garden Cottage was something else. As Lisa and Dick walked down the steps from the road, they saw the garden spreading out below and said "Oh yes!" As the cottage door opened, the big old beams came immediately into view. "That's it!" said Lisa, and so it was.

It was immediately clear that Garden Cottage was going to be too small to serve as their only residence and so they were soon beginning to think about how they might improve it. "We had lots of ideas", Dick recalls. "Much of what we have done was about making the place more 'user friendly' while creating a little more space both downstairs and upstairs."

Inevitably there were aspects of the premises that they wanted to tackle quickly - not the least of which was replacing the lean-to that had housed the boiler and washing machine. This work would become stage one.

But from the outset they planned a fuller enhancement with the intention of

Above:
Stage One: Construction of the new extension on the north-west side of Garden Cottage in place of the previous "lean-to".

implementing it as stage two when their Cambridge property had been sold and extra funds provided from the proceeds.

And so Oliver Dicks soon had another assignment. The Robinsons cannot remember when or how they first met with Oliver although in their case it wasn't in a pub. One of their first reactions was to wonder whether Oliver was actually an architect - which of course he wasn't - and whether this would become an issue. But soon they recognised his talents. "We felt comfortable if Ollie was happy with our plans", Dick recalls. "He understood the engineering bit. And he knew everyone in the planning department which helped smooth the way."

As a project, Garden Cottage had a couple of built-in advantages. First, it was not a listed building. And secondly it had Dick's readiness to roll up his sleeves and work on the building himself. This stemmed from the time the Robinsons moved to Suffolk in the nineteen seventies and Dick first got involved in refurbishing a property. Now, with 12 house moves and several renovations under his belt, he was eager to start on Garden Cottage himself and prove that he could still do it.

Given that background it is not surprising that most of the ideas would originate with Dick and Lisa Robinson, although there was not always an immediate consensus between them. Dick's first wish was to build a big extension in front of the existing entrance. But Lisa was able to temper his enthusiasm. The outcome was more modest and preserved much of the original frontage. As we shall see, those initial plans would be subject to further revision as Dick and Lisa continued to have further and better thoughts.

Meanwhile work started on stage one. It had been preceded by a debate about the pitch of the lean-to roof which had never matched that of the main house. In the end everyone agreed to adhere to the existing pitch when rebuild-

Right:
Oliver's drawings showing the previous ground floor layout of Garden Cottage and how it would be extended and altered.

ing and heightening the extension, rather than risk restricting the view from the adjacent property. The plan for stage one was for the lean-to to be replaced by a ground floor bedroom/reception room and bathroom, accessed from what had been the lounge. The wall between the lounge and kitchen would be demolished. The lounge fireplace would be removed and replaced by French doors opening out to the garden.

It took Dick about 10 months to construct the extension and other works, helped by Don Hicks who was a skilled builder. But the project was not without its moment of drama. The removal of the lounge fireplace required the insertion of a steel joist to support the external wall above. Oliver sought out a structural engineer to advise. After that, Dick and Don decided to lift the joist into place between them, propping it up with bricks as they did so. "I still have sleepless nights recalling it", Dick says. Inch by inch the joist was lifted until eventually it was in its appointed resting place and the wall above was secure: "When we told Ollie, he was pretty amazed."

With stage one completed in 2002, attention turned to the bigger project that was to follow as stage two.

This involved extensions and modifications that would expand the living space on the ground floor and provide a study and a bigger bathroom on the first floor. Inevitably initial thoughts were revisited and revised. And Oliver was constantly on the receiving end of them. Lisa was surprised that Oliver never seemed bored by yet another idea or alteration. "I'll just go and have a look on my computer", he would say, and a little later Dick and Lisa would join him. They would spend many hours with Oliver as he grabbed components in the drawings and moved them around the computer screen.

"We would thrash it out together", says Lisa, "with laughter, disapproval,

Above:
The enlarged front entrance on the south-east side of Garden Cottage (see also the drawings below).

Before   After

Render

Left:
Oliver Dick's drawings of the south-east side which formed the front of Garden Cottage before and after the proposed alterations.

57

objection or wild agreement. He made it such fun."

Dick reckons a session with Oliver was not for the faint hearted: "There was lots of argy-bargy, yet he was almost as keen on the project as we were. If we disagreed, by the next day all was well and Ollie was his normal chatty self."

"He liked the challenge of the argument. It was all part of the fun", says Lisa. "He had strong views, and he made sure we knew them. But he was always approachable. We could phone him at 9am on a Sunday morning and he would always say: 'It's not a problem'."

Oliver suggested positioning the rear wall of the main extension as close to the boundary with the Robinsons' neighbours as was legally permissible, thereby creating more internal space. Then they decided to relocate the kitchen to where the dining room had been and to extend that room towards the garden (see plans on previous pages). This enabled the lounge to be extended back to occupy the space where the kitchen had previously been and for a new fireplace to be built into the west wall.

But any extension of the new kitchen/dining area into the garden threatened to put the adjacent patio into the shade. Oliver took great pleasure in using his computer software to demonstrate how to adjust the pitch of the new roof to minimise any shadow.

By 2006 all the extensions and modifications had been completed. And what gave the Robinsons greatest satisfaction? In Lisa's view it was the "gentle transformation" of the cottage - which doesn't really impact on its original looks. It's not the first time such a tribute has been expressed in this book.

Vale Cottage

Vale Cottage was the home of Oliver Dicks' mother Olwen until she died in July 1999[14]. It stands alongside Blockley Brook at the junction with Donkey Lane at the Dovedale end of the High Street.

Initially Oliver and Jean had not given any thought to moving there themselves as it had only two bedrooms whereas their home in Northwick Terrace had four. Then they began to think about building an extra room above the cottage's kitchen with access from the landing, but Oliver concluded that the foundations were not strong enough to carry the extra load.

A little later their daughter Kate asked the obvious question: "Why do we need more than two bedrooms?" The solution was a practical compromise: as Oliver would need one room as an office, this could double as a bed-sitting room if and when the need arose.

Opposite page:
The well-trodden path to Oliver Dicks' study in Vale Cottage where he would often be seen looking out of the window (bottom left) or poring over his computer. Vale Cottage was refurbished by Oliver for his family after his mother died.

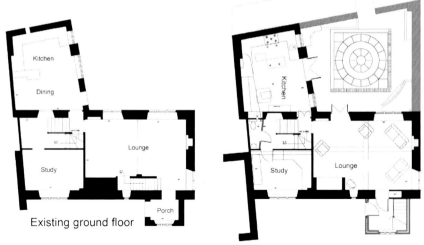

Existing ground floor

Proposed ground floor

"Once committed, Oliver was determined to do it properly", Jean recalls. "We spent many hours wandering around the property and discussing what we could do. As we did so, our ideas slowly developed." Oliver would return to his computer and draw those ideas with Jean looking over his shoulder: "It was very exciting and the first time I had become personally involved with Oliver's work."

Structural changes were planned for the front of the property: the porch would be demolished and replaced by a larger one - using the original mullioned window and door, but allowing room for a new staircase to be constructed leading to the first floor. The existing staircase would be removed, opening up a larger lounge (see drawings). And the lounge would feel even larger when a bricked-up fireplace - something that Oliver had always been aware of - could be opened up again and brought back into use.

Oliver designed a patio leading from the rear of the house to the brook, accessed through new French doors from both the lounge and the kitchen/dining room. Then Jean and Oliver turned their attention to the kitchen and dining area itself. They decided to raise the floor level to avoid stepping down into it. The kitchen ceiling would be boxed in and two skylights added. "We really transformed the kitchen", Jean says with the obvious pleasure of someone who is an enthusiastic cook. "It's now very sunny with the patio forming a natural extension to it."

Other alterations they planned together included the construction of a toilet on the existing first floor landing at the north-east end of the property (this is at the opposite end of the building to the front porch as there are two separate staircases). Beneath it, what had previously been a coal store would be replaced by a second entrance hall and a new utility room. Oliver also remodelled and enlarged the guest bathroom, and redesigned the access from the second bedroom to its en-suite bathroom in the eaves of the building. The roof timbers were found to be rotten above the guest bathroom and so the opportunity was taken to increase the size of the window when the roof timbers were replaced.

With the plans approved the property was cleared in the Spring of 2000 so that building work could begin. "On the surface it looked great", Jean recalls, "but once they started knocking it about, it became clear that quite a lot of the floorboards would have to be replaced. At one stage during the building work you could see from the ground floor right up to the roof." A particularly vulnerable area was around the "walk in" bath Oliver's mother had installed. When it was dismantled the flooring was found to be rotten. "I can't believe she never fell through", a surprised Oliver said at the time.

Jean took a particularly keen interest in the kitchen. None of the old walls were straight and so all the kitchen furniture had to be hand built: "We had looked at professional kitchen designers, but in the end we created our own design. We planned to have a marble topped island unit, but after it was built we didn't like it. Part of it was converted into a dresser." At an earlier stage Jean remembers going into the house one day and finding power points all along a wall. "What have the electricians done?" she enquired. It was quite obvious that they hadn't looked at the plans.

Once the house had been redesigned, attention turned to finding a way to get the Dicks' cars off the road. Oliver came up with the idea of building a platform at the front of the garden with a store room beneath. But the planners

Existing first floor

Proposed first floor

Above:
Oliver's drawings for first floor of Vale Cottage.
Below (left to right):
The original lounge fireplace rediscovered (note previous staircase to left); Rebuilding the lounge fireplace; Installing the French windows in the kitchen.

Opposite page:
Rear view of the terrace of cottages known as Rose Row that back on to the left of the High Street when approaching Dovedale woods. Rosedale is on the left and Meadowbrook is just right of centre.

would not allow the garden wall to be knocked down. On reflection Oliver thought it would have cost a lot of money and he was never totally comfortable about the impact it would have had on drainage.

The final element of the renovation was the garden. Jean and Oliver called on the services of Marion Leslie to help them. Mindful that Oliver's mother had been a great gardener, evidenced by her influence on the gardens at The Old Silk Mill when she had lived there, Jean thought long and hard before taking out any of her plants: "We kept much of the original planting, including the Golden Yew. She would have been very pleased."

However, there was one aspect of the front garden design that might have caused tension. The plan was for the terrace to be curved, but Oliver had a different view, exclaiming bluntly: "You can't do that!" Whether the builders simply thought it would be easier to build a straight wall remains a mystery, but Oliver discussed it with Marion and came to an amicable agreement. Oliver's view prevailed.

Rosedale

Just before reaching the junction that leads off to The Warren and opposite Vine Cottage[15] there stands a terrace of cottages facing away from the High Street towards the south east.

The terrace is called Rose Row and probably qualifies for an award as the dullest and longest stretch of wall in the entire Cotswolds. Folklore tells how Lady Northwick insisted that the cottages should not have any windows facing the road so as to protect her privacy when her carriage passed on the way to or from Dovedale House. Equally plausible would be a desire to build the cottages so that they faced the nearby Blockley Brook and the hill beyond, thereby offering a far more appealing view to residents.

Oliver contributed to the refurbishment of two cottages in Rose Row. The first to benefit from his wisdom and skills stands at the Dovedale end of the Row and is called Rosedale. At an earlier stage in its life this property had been

Right:
Oliver Dick's plans for extending the first floor of Rosedale at the southern end of Rose Row.

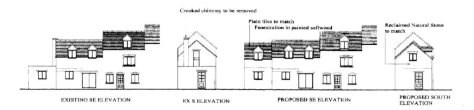

EXISTING SE ELEVATION   EX S ELEVATION   PROPOSED SE ELEVATION   PROPOSED SOUTH ELEVATION

enlarged by combining what originally had been two smaller cottages and there-after it had been occupied by a well-loved local resident Celia Serpell. After she died, the property came on the market and attracted the attention of a journalist Pam Merritt who had also been living in the village for some years.

Pam bought Rosedale in 2006, having decided she would like to split the property back into two cottages again and retain the end unit for herself. At the same time she would extend the first floor above the single storey utility room so as to provide a larger and more modern bathroom. She also decided to merge the existing "snug" with the kitchen, creating much more working space. Almost inevitably the property was in need of general upgrading and this too formed part of the plan.

Involving Oliver in the process was an obvious choice: "He knew all about houses and the pitfalls, and I knew him!"

The biggest challenge came from an unseen source - the drains. It quickly became clear that they didn't go where Severn Trent Water thought they went. So Oliver had to redraw a map showing their true location. According to Pam, Oliver was "absolutely indispensible", and she recalls some fierce debates between him and Severn Trent's water engineers.

Oliver was also typically firm with his views about the roof line of the first floor extension, insisting correctly that the planners would require it to drop below the adjacent roof line so as to continue the profile already established with the neighbouring cottages (see drawing on page 62)[16].

The building work was carried out in two stages, with the first floor extension forming the second segment. The first stage involved separating the two cottages, removing a downstairs cloakroom and creating the larger kitchen, after which Pam moved in. The advantages were immediately obvious - more room and more light.

The builder Henry Goodrick-Clarke was "a star", Pam says, while repeating the widely expressed view that Oliver was always generous with his time: "He would sit at his computer huffing and puffing because the printer refused to work." Then in a pained tone of voice that is less than convincing she adds: "But he never offered me a gin and tonic!" Pam must feel she was the only person in Blockley to have been deprived in this way. However the friendship never diminished. Throughout the project she would be very tentative about asking Oliver to do things in case she abused that friendship. And with Oliver's continuing reluctance to accept any financial reward, Pam would be seen stalking him at local wine-tastings, making a note of what he liked best…

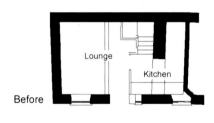

Before

After

Above:
Oliver Dicks' drawings of Meadowbrook's
ground floor before and after its redesign.

The final part of the building work was completed in the summer of 2007. Two weeks later, the refurbished ground floor was temporarily submerged by the widespread flooding that hit the north Cotswolds after an unusually heavy rainfall.

Meadowbrook

Midway along Rose Row a narrow alleyway leads from the lane to a cottage known now as Meadowbrook. The stone wall leading to the alley bears scars left behind by the US military from World War II. According to local residents, some boisterous soldiers - armed with little more than an excessive consumption of alcohol - attempted to drive their jeep down the passageway until it eventually dawned upon them that it would be necessary either to widen the alley or shrink the jeep[17].

The cottage had been left empty for many years before Mark and Shirley Penfold found it in 2003. They had been looking to move from Little Compton to Blockley for some time as Mark had fond memories of the village from the age of about eight when he used to visit his grandmother here.

"It was the first property we looked at", Mark recalls. "It had very little furniture and what there was had a distinctive 'fifties' feel about it. It was also very damp, dark and dingy, but we knew it had potential."

Mark already knew Oliver Dicks quite well and had mentioned to him their desire to find a home. Oliver's response was typical: "Before you make an offer, let me go round and take a look." So he did. The Penfolds could see what needed changing to bring the property up to date and provide a more appealing living space. There were three good sized bedrooms upstairs, but only a very tiny bathroom. Downstairs was dark and very small. So it would benefit from an extension to the rear that provided space for a modern kitchen and a cloakroom. The first floor also needed reconfiguring to provide a larger bathroom.

Right:
The South-east elevation of Meadowbrook
(facing the brook) before and after redesign.

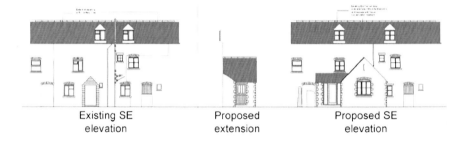

Existing SE
elevation

Proposed
extension

Proposed SE
elevation

The brief to Oliver was to come up with a plan that would satisfy Mark and Shirley's needs and be acceptable to the planning authorities. Mark tells how Oliver went away and very soon came back with the plan: "We looked at it and said 'OK'."

Observers may be surprised to notice how the extension interrupts the smooth line of cottages as seen from the rear and from upper Dovedale. Apparently the cottages are not listed buildings and the planners raised no objections. However, getting planning consent soon seemed the least of the Penfolds' worries as they began to prepare for the extension's foundations to be laid.

Working with two builder friends, Mark started digging. And digging. And digging. Six feet down there was still soft clay - as well as the skull of a long deceased cow. They discovered that Rose Row had been built on the edge of dew ponds which had been obscured many years ago by Lady Northwick's landscaping activities.

"It was getting very dangerous", Mark explains. So, after taking further advice, it was decided that piles would be required. A total of 12 piles were each sunk 27 feet into the clay, and all to support a single storey extension. According to Mark, one pile alone would have been able to withstand 12 tonnes of pressure and the entire extension did not weigh that much: "So now our extension is probably holding up the whole of Rose Row."

Another unnerving experience related to the builders' tools. Each night they would put them away, taking careful note of where they were placed. But on their return next morning, the tools were in different places. The ghostly explanation was that the mole-catcher's grand-dad used to live in the house and was known as a practical joker.

Dovedale Cottage

Approaching the entrance to Dovedale woods, a cottage has stood at right angles to the lane for several centuries. Unsurprisingly it is called Dovedale Cottage and was bought by Eleanor McLauchlan in 1972 as a country retreat from Birmingham after her father orthopaedic surgeon Bill Scrase had discovered the property through friends.

Eleanor's husband Robert had a healthcare distribution business in Birmingham and so they made limited use of the cottage initially and for a while it was made available for holiday letting. In 2005, after Robert sold his business and was no longer tied to his Birmingham office, he and Eleanor came to stay at Dovedale Cottage. "We decided very fast that it made most sense to restore and

Below:
Dovedale Cottage looking north towards the High Street before alterations.

Opposite page:
Front of Dovedale Cottage before work began

extend the property, and to move to Blockley full-time", Robert recalls.

Intent on getting rid of some of their less appealing possessions, Robert and Eleanor organised a house contents sale which was to lead them very quickly to Oliver Dicks. Attending the sale were near neighbours Mark and Shirley Penfold who, on hearing of the McLauchlan's plans, explained that the chap they needed to see lived just a few doors down the lane. "If he likes the idea and likes you, he might do it", Mark said. A neighbour Malcolm Sinclair walked them to Oliver's house and he came round that very afternoon.

"He was very very good", says Robert who quickly took a liking to him. "He was not like the typical architect I had been used to. He was receptive and creative, and he knew what would satisfy the planners." However, it was not always clear whether Oliver's occasional assertion that a particular idea "would never get through the planners" was entirely motivated by his planning knowledge, rather than by a particular aversion to the idea itself.

Discussions progressed and at a subsequent meeting Oliver was able to demonstrate how badly the property had deteriorated when most of one leg disappeared through the bedroom floor. "This place is as rotten as a pear", he exclaimed with feeling. And he was right. The discovery was to knock a hole in the McLauchlan's confidence as well as in their bank balance. What had been envisaged as a simple extension job now became a major rebuilding project. Virtually all the interior had to be gutted and replaced. Only two external walls would remain untouched.

Below:
Dovedale Cottage extension plan with original external walls highlighted in darker shade.

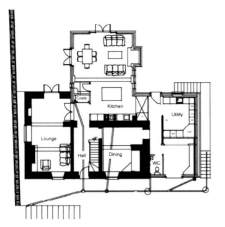

As soon as Oliver had completed his first drawings, Robert and Eleanor went to his house to see them. It was about 4pm. Hospitable as ever, Oliver offered them each a drink - or to be more precise, a lot of drink - in which the quantity of tonic water was kept to a minimum so as not to spoil the flavour of the Plymouth gin. It was not long before the McLauchlans were to regret not having had any lunch. To this day they do not recall how they got home again.

The plan involved removing all of the rotted interior and extending the premises to the south-west in a T-shape.

The extension would house a new open kitchen and seating area leading out through French doors to the rear garden. Above there would be a new master bedroom and ensuite bathroom. The existing kitchen - housed in a "lean-to" structure attached to the north-west of the original building - would be replaced by a newly-built utility room and study, above which another additional bedroom would be added.

The result would be a six bedroomed spacious home instead of a "two up,

Opposite (left to right):
Oliver Dicks and Eleanor McLauchlan
survey the rear of the old cottage;
Interior after removing rotten flooring;
Cut away at the rear showing condition of
floors;
Construction workers wrestle with spring
water flowing across the site;
Almost complete - the rear of the cottage as
it looks today (and which can be compared
with the picture on page 67).

two down" cottage, and the transformation would take the best part of three years to complete.

The original cottage was built on rock, or at least most of it was. At each end of the building the rock gave way to "brash" - broken rock and less stable materials. The original builders must have known what they were doing because, the further the distance from the house, the less stable the ground becomes. Alert to this possibility, Oliver recommended a geotechnical survey of the site. The findings were of limited value and failed to disclose the extent to which water flowed beneath the ground. But the survey did establish the presence of blue clay at the furthest distance from the lane.

Eleanor's father knew that water flowed beneath the cottage. He could hear it. His only difficulty had been in discovering where it came from.

It did not take the builders very long to find the answer. Before building could commence, surplus soil had to be removed from the site to make way for the foundations. It took 120 journeys by 18-tonne trucks to complete the task. And, as they did so, water took its place. With nowhere else to go, the back garden soon resembled a swimming pool, fed by Blockley's natural springs. Fortunately, it was not long before the problem could be solved. A slab of concrete had blocked an old culvert that used to allow water to flow away from the site alongside the wall that abuts the lane. Once the slab had been removed, a yellow stream began to emerge from the site and flow down the brook. In due course the springs would be landscaped to form a natural stream flowing alongside the patio at the rear of the house.

To provide stable foundations for the extension, piles were driven 27 feet

into the brash. When the foundations were in place, work started on removing some of the existing walls, stripping away internal plasterwork and extracting rotten timbers. Some external walls needed little help to take down as they were prone to collapse of their own accord. Insofar as old timbers had not rotted they were reinstated later alongside the new. Wherever possible existing rooms were restored to their original appearance and the atmosphere of an old cottage retained.

The installation of more modern amenities in the extension was not achieved without a certain amount of trauma. For example, the underfloor heating was installed with such enthusiasm that it extended beneath the pantry and the fireplace. Oliver quickly had this remedied.

The overall verdict? "The flow of the house is fantastic", enthuses Eleanor. "It's a wonderful home to live in and the planning was brilliant."

And the biggest disappointment? Robert says it was discovering at the outset that they could not do the simple extension they had intended. And on reflection perhaps also he would have avoided using new stone instead of old for the extension. "But I am extremely pleased with the house", says Robert. "You can hardly tell that it is a complete rebuild and most visitors have no idea."

On the Friday before Oliver died, he came to show Robert and Eleanor some slides of his cruise on Fred Olsen's *Braemar*. It was a happy evening despite Oliver's obvious discomfort. "I feel guilty about your house", he said, looking towards the French doors. But he never explained why. Maybe he realised the doors had not been made tall enough to readily accommodate Robert's height.

CHAPTER 6

Hotels and Hostelries

"Oliver then went round looking elsewhere at the stonework and 'read' their possible earlier uses and locations: it revealed an amazing knowledge of, and empathy with, the building history of a past age."

In its heyday Blockley boasted seven ale houses, inns and hotels. Only two remain today and, as will already have become evident, Oliver Dicks knew them both very well. Not only did Oliver partake of their hospitality, but he applied his design talents to the premises too. His design contribution extended beyond the two remaining hostelries to include two other establishments where pints were no longer being pulled.

The Red Lion was one such abandoned ale house, owned now by Don and Irene Jowett. It will be found at the Dovedale end of the High Street alongside a raised footpath. The remnants of some painted lettering can still be seen on the front wall as evidence of its former life.

The Jowetts bought 1 Red Lion Steps, as it is now called, in 1994. Oliver was not involved in preparing the refurbishment plan itself, but he gave valuable advice on three aspects. He suggested reducing the first floor landing area and combining the existing bathroom and separate toilet so as to provide an en suite facility to the main bedroom. This created the added benefit of increasing the size of the second bedroom. He also helped design a new rear staircase that allowed a toilet and laundry area to be created on the ground floor beneath it. And he suggested the removal of the "vault" between the kitchen and sitting room on the ground floor and the erection of a load bearing stud wall in its place, thereby increasing the size of the kitchen significantly.

In addition, Oliver was able to confirm that the work would not require planning permission (the building was not listed) and to ratify the structural viability of all the changes. In Don's words: "When talking to us in his typically bluff, forthright way, he never suggested for one moment that rules were there

Opposite page:
Red Lion Steps and the former Red Lion inn after refurbishment for Don and Irene Jowett.
Below:
The residue of a sign painted on the wall of The Red Lion (Photograph: Gay Thompson)

Photograph: Tony Skellett

to be bent or by-passed.   His assured manner was not bluster - his confidence was based simply on precise knowledge and a wealth of experience."

When Oliver was inspecting the area on the ground floor at the back of the house, he was mystified that it didn't contain a small fireplace in the rear wall, as he would have expected this part of the building to have provided a "snug" area comprising a kitchen and sitting room to which the pub's owners and staff could retreat.   However, he concluded this was an impossibility as there was no chimney above it.   Instead there was a huge single plate glass window in what had been a studio for the previous owner Nora Yoxall.   Some time later, when builder Alan Warburton was clearing the area, he pulled aside a large piece of boarding, prompting an avalanche of mud and rubble: lo and behold, there was a fireplace, with the remains of a blocked off chimney behind it!

Around another old fireplace, in the kitchen, there were several quite deep holes and slots in the stonework. Don and Irene asked Oliver what their function might have been when the old kitchen's equipment had been in place. "In some cases the holes had nothing to do with the current building but probably predated its construction", Oliver explained. "The stones might previously have been used as gateposts with the holes forming part of the original hinges. In those days they didn't believe in wasting a good bit of stone!"   Don tells how Oliver then went round looking elsewhere at the stonework and "read" their possible earlier uses and locations: "It revealed an amazing knowledge of, and empathy with, the building history of a past age."

The Great Western Arms

Another public house that benefitted from Oliver's advice was *The Great Western Arms*. Apart from *The Crown* hotel, it is the only public house still serving the village and Oliver spent quite a lot of time there over the years. John and Liz Ferguson took over the tenancy in September 1988 and by the early nineteen nineties they were in discussions with the Hook Norton brewery about a major refurbishment.

The plan was to provide a larger kitchen to replace its predecessor that John Ferguson describes as a "tiny cupboard" in part of the area that is now the public bar. It is hard to imagine how any meals could have been prepared in such a small space. This part of the refurbishment plan also involved moving the toilets downstairs to the lower ground floor.

John Ferguson tells how Oliver would be sitting on his bar stool listening to design discussions with the Hook Norton architect and would interject with

Photograph: Tony Skellett

Opposite page:
The Old Royal Oak as it looks today

some highly practical pieces of advice. Did he have many suggestions? "Stacks of them", says John. "He was fantastic. The brewery's architect went along with everything he proposed." The drawings would then be updated to reflect Oliver's suggestions - but without attribution!

A couple of Oliver inspired changes are still remembered. One was to reject the architect's plan for a straight bar to run the whole length of the lounge, despite having taken delivery of the oak top. Oliver said it would create a better atmosphere if it was replaced by an L-shaped arrangement. And it was.

Then there was the plan to insert French windows leading from the lounge to the car park: "It won't work", said Oliver, and it never happened.

John describes how Oliver was involved in other ways too: "A couple of times he stopped the builders by saying in characteristic style 'You can't do that!'. It got to the stage where the builder would arrive in the morning and ask 'What have I got to change this time?'. It was a nightmare keeping the pub open while all this was going on."

The Royal Oak

As its name implies, *The Royal Oak* was one of a number of alehouses that supplied the wants of Blockley villagers for more than a century. The property forms part of a terrace in the High Street that is fronted by a raised footpath and looks down towards School Lane. Before the terrace was built there were already one or two smaller properties situated a little further away from the roadside at the foot of a field leading up to Bell Bank.

Among them was a small double-fronted cottage built at (roughly) right angles to the High Street with its front door facing north-east rather than towards the street below. Its original structure dates from the late seventeenth or early eighteenth century and much of it remains today, including the flagstones forming the ground floor and broad elm planks that form the first floor above. A timber framed partition wall has also been retained on the first floor.

When the more imposing terrace was constructed about a century later the original cottage was incorporated into it to form part of what became *The Royal Oak*. It closed as an alehouse in 1955 when the brewery surrendered its licence. The property was then renamed The Old Royal Oak and served for a while as a fruiterer and florist, trading as A J Worthington. Later it was purchased by Sir Edward and Lady Grizel Warner. Sir Edward was a retired ambassador whose family had earlier connections with Blockley and, after moving into the village, he became the president of what is now The Blockley Heritage Society[18].

Below:
The Royal Oak alehouse in 1907- on the right of the picture looking south-west towards Dovedale.

Sir Edward died in 2002 and shortly afterwards his elderly widow decided she would like to move nearer to some of her remaining family in Scotland. By this time their neighbours in Vine House were Rob and Carol Willott who, after their second marriage, were in need of a larger property to house their extended family encompassing three generations. "It seemed too much of a coincidence to ignore", Carol recalls, "although we suspected the property would need a lot of refurbishment and modification, not least because my mother was 93 years old and would have to be accommodated on the ground floor." As a Grade II listed building in a conservation area it was not clear how much alteration would be permitted. For example, the two outside toilets that had been erected at the rear for patrons of the alehouse were derelict and redundant.

Oliver Dicks was the obvious person to consult. Would it be possible to create a four-bedroom property, with a study, a self-contained ground floor bed/sitting room and shower room, and all the normal living rooms? And could the design allow the bed-sitting room to revert to a conventional lounge at a future date? Unless these requirements could be achieved, it would not have been worth proceeding with the purchase and so any offer had to be made subject to gaining planning consent. In this respect Lady Warner was unceasingly sympathetic and patient.

Oliver arrived with his tape measure and soon the layout had been loaded on to his computer in its existing configuration. Later that day he returned with his first ideas about redesigning the property. But even as he was about to explain them, his brain was conjuring up further permutations. So he apologised and, without showing any of his drawings, he returned home to his computer and within hours was back again with another version.

Left to right:
The Old Royal Oak's rear courtyard when purchased, with outside toilets for patrons; the courtyard after demolition of outbuildings; the courtyard today, designed by Paul Williams.

Oliver's initial plans were both imaginative and practical. The ground floor proposals took advantage of the fact that the original building had no internal load-bearing walls and such internal walls as there were had been constructed relatively recently. The original stone passageway through the centre of the house from the front door to the back would literally be ripped up. This would allow the original bar area to be enlarged to form the bed/sitting room required for Carol's mother. The front entrance would remain, but a small lobby would be created inside it leading leftwards into a sizeable hall/library. The existing staircase would be turned from its previous route so as to lead down into the new hall, making it a major feature of the refurbishment. This would also provide space for a new shower room to be constructed on the ground floor.

A new kitchen would be built at the rear of the property where a tap room had once served the public bar. This would enable the existing kitchen, located on the ground floor of the original cottage, to be converted into a dining room that would convey the atmosphere and character of the old building to best effect.

The first floor would be reconfigured to comprise a guest bedroom, a family bathroom, a master bedroom with en-suite bathroom and a study/bedroom. The second floor would be converted into two bedrooms and another bathroom for Carol's daughters when they returned home from university studies.

On Oliver's advice a meeting was arranged with a conservation officer in May 2002 to establish in broad terms whether any aspect of the proposals was likely to meet with official opposition. The meeting went well, although some relatively minor changes were made as a result. But when the plans were submitted, the conservation officer objected to several aspects and so Oliver arranged

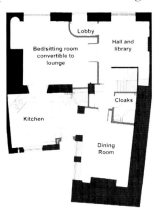

Left:
The ground floor of The Old Royal Oak before alteration.

Right:
The ground floor as finally redesigned to satisfy the planners (- the staircase no longer leads down to the hall as Oliver initially had wanted).

a site meeting to discuss them. The two most problematic features were proposed alterations to the staircase and to the upper floors. The conservation officer refused to contemplate turning the staircase down into the new hall, as proposed, on the grounds that the existing staircase was comprised of original timber. While it may well have been true that the timbers were original, it was quite obvious that they were not in their original position. When originally built, the staircase would have been formed of a single flight from the central passageway to the first floor. The remains of the first floor landing are visible still.

But the conservation officer would not budge. His attention then turned to the first floor partition walls. He wanted to know which were comprised of original lath and plaster as understandably he would have wished them to be preserved. Oliver could not contain his irritation. In his view any half competent conservation officer or surveyor could establish the nature of the walls by looking at them and/or tapping on them with his hand. But the conservation officer wanted holes to be drilled in the walls to establish their composition. To this suggestion there was one rather obvious reply: as the Willotts had not bought the property yet, it seemed unreasonable to expect Lady Warner to agree to holes being drilled in her walls.

Nothing further was heard from the conservation officer or the planning department. Many weeks passed as Lady Warner waited patiently to know whether or not she had a firm buyer. By October 2002 the Willotts had decided that the only fair course of action was to withdraw their offer so that Lady Warner could seek another buyer rather than be delayed further in her desire to move. Through her agent she kindly offered to adjust the price if the deal could still go ahead. When the situation was relayed to Oliver, he immediately rose to the challenge. "Let's see whether we can modify the plans in an acceptable manner and get them approved", he volunteered.

Reluctantly the idea of a feature staircase was abandoned and various other minor design features were amended to minimise the risk of rejection. Within 24 hours the revised plans had been submitted, only to be greeted again by a deafening silence.

After several more weeks an exasperated Rob Willott phoned the planning officer, explained his predicament and asked what was causing the delay. The officer involved was very helpful: "If you can send me a letter today confirming the nature and origin of partitions to be removed and that none of the alterations will have a detrimental effect on load-bearing walls, I will undertake to pass the plans before I leave for a holiday at the end of the week." Oliver pointed out that the only partition walls being removed were those of plasterboard construction inserted on the ground floor in the nineteen sixties and that self-evidently there were no load-bearing walls inside the property. It was easy to provide the required assurances. Within 48 hours, planning consent had been granted.

The first stage of the refurbishment involved stripping out much of the existing internal fabric on the ground floor as well as all the existing electrical and plumbing work. The outside toilets and other outbuildings were also demolished. "The place looked as if a bomb had hit it", Carol recalls.

During this preliminary work a number of significant discoveries were made. It became clear that one of the main joists supporting the top floor was rotten and would have to be replaced. Then it was discovered that a cupboard had been built into part of the space that originally would have formed the first floor landing. By removing this cupboard and another constructed beneath, it would be possible to open up the stair well from ground floor to the roof allowing natural light to flood down from above. Oliver was able to turn this discovery into a delightful feature on each half landing.

Stripping away the kitchen furniture to create the new dining room revealed an original stone fireplace. However, at first sight the fireplace seemed to have been set back behind the line of the wall itself. On closer examination it transpired that the rear wall of the room in which the fireplace had originally been constructed had been reinforced on the inside at a later date by the building of an additional wall. Fortunately the chimney was still accessible and so Oliver recommended building a new stone fireplace in front of the original one.

An examination of the tap room lead to a couple of unexpected benefits. First it proved possible to reopen access to the former bar that had been bricked up when the hostelry closed. The opening provided a perfect hatchway from the new kitchen through to the bed/sitting room that would eventually revert to

Below (left to right):
Demolition begins -"the place looked as if a bomb had hit it"; The gutted tap room; The new kitchen built on the site of the old tap room (the hatch on the right is on the site of the original bar); The new dining room fireplace built in front of the previous one.

Opposite page:
The Crown Inn & Hotel as it looks today.
The former bank and bakery businesses
occupied the area behind the two bay windows
on the left.

a lounge. Readers may be disappointed to learn that a restrictive covenant imposed by the Flowers brewery prevents beer being sold from the reopened bar these days, but presumably it can still be given away. The tap room also housed the boiler that had provided hot water and central heating. The building contractors were of the opinion that the boiler was in good condition and large enough to satisfy the demands of the refurbished property. So it was salvaged and relocated upstairs alongside a new *Megaflow* hot water storage cylinder.

Oliver made a number of other valuable contributions to the refurbishment. One related to how the top floor was reached from the staircase. Previously access could only be achieved by bending over and creeping through a very low door. Oliver redesigned the staircase so that it turned towards the apex of the roof, allowing easy access even by those of above average height.

Another notable contribution can be seen in the new hall and library. For this Oliver was able to source the construction of wall panelling, matching cupboards and bookshelves to his own design. So although the planners deprived Oliver of the staircase he had hoped would make an impact on entering the hall, an attractive memorial to his talent has been left in that room.

And for what will Oliver be best remembered? "His diligence, enthusiasm and imagination", says Carol, "and most of all for his unwavering support." There is one other memento that Oliver left at The Old Royal Oak: four light fittings set into the kitchen ceiling about 16 feet above floor level. Each time a bulb has to be replaced, Oliver is remembered.

The Crown

The largest hostelry in Blockley has already featured frequently in these pages. It is *The Crown* and it stands out quite distinctively in the High Street as a former coaching inn. But in the nineteen eighties it was a much smaller place. The entrance was on the left-hand side of the drive under the archway and it lead directly into the public bar.

In 1986 the property was bought by Jim Champion when his family moved down from London. The Champions evidently had ambitions to put *The Crown* on the map both as an eating place and a country house hotel. Using London architects The Broad & Bennett Partnership, plans were drawn up and planning consent obtained to create a new restaurant, kitchen and bedrooms to replace a function room, skittle alley and outbuildings beyond the entrance archway. However, the Champions' ambitions did not end there. By November 1986 two adjacent buildings had been acquired - a former bakery and the former branch

Below:
The Crown (to the right of the picture) before the
Champions bought it and extended the premises to
incorporate the adjacent shops (centre).

of Lloyd's Bank - and plans submitted by the same architects to convert this area into about 12 additional bedrooms on three floors with an extension to the rear. For reasons that have not been documented, the ground floor area never became bedrooms[19], but instead became a popular bistro with a reputation for its fish menu that spread for miles around. In due course *The Crown* would become the place where London incomers and locals alike would meet and eat until replete.

By this time Oliver Dicks was to be found regularly in the bar with local builders Simon Bolton and Alan Warburton. They soon became involved in discussions with the Champions and their architects about their expansion plans and, as if by osmosis, it was not long before they found themselves engaged more practically on the building alterations. "It was sort of assumed that we would do it", Simon recalls. He remembers walking through the deserted bakery among redundant tables, dated newspapers and other debris. By contrast the bank had been emptied completely. Architect Alan Bennett still remembers a number of suggestions being made by Oliver, some of which lead to further modifications to the plans, although no evidence has been found of any drawings produced by Oliver himself. Some amended drawings did find their way to the council planning department, but without attribution other than being described as revisions to the earlier plans.[19]

By 1988 work was in progress to link the old bank and bakery premises with the original inn. To create space for the rear extension, it was necessary to remove a lot of earth and to replace it with concrete foundations. That was not as simple as it may seem. The only access was from the rear of the site which in those days backed on to Chapel Lane. Simon Bolton tells how a Hymac digger was offloaded in Chapel Lane and then progressed gingerly down the hill to-

Right:
Revision to architects' drawings for the rear of The Crown creating a landing exit (left) and (right) illustration based on the architects' original ground floor plan envisaging additional bedrooms where the bistro was eventually built.

wards the back of *The Crown*. The digger was used to claw back the soil while concrete was tipped into the trench from ordinary buckets. "I was the only person down there, while above me was the precariously postured Hymac", Simon explains, and then adds as an afterthought: "There was no sign of Ollie." Instead Oliver would appear in the bar each evening on the way home from his Wychavon day job (Oliver was still employed by the council at this time) and a congenial discussion would ensue with the Champions, Simon and Alan on the work in progress.

As the project progressed, Simon applied his considerable carpentry skills to the construction of room dividers that among other functions would provide corridors leading from the bar into the bistro. Each divider comprised a wooden lower panel with a "grill" section above. Transporting these panels from Simon's workshop at Northwick Park to their final resting place was a precarious exercise in itself, as they overhung the perimeter of his van. But they proved to be a perfect fit. Too perfect. Most had to be eased into place with a little more energy than might have seemed prudent, causing the ceiling to rise upwards by a few millimetres while Jim Champion looked on anxiously.

Eventually the work was completed and the opening night was celebrated with a grand dinner. Accompanied by their wives, Oliver, Simon and Alan were guests at the Champions' table. Just as the festivities began, the entire hotel was plunged into a total blackout, much to the embarrassment of everyone on the Champion's table. An electrician had to be called and fortunately the cause was traced to a dishwasher fuse. Thereafter the bistro prospered for a number of years, giving great satisfaction to everyone involved. But the world moves on and the Champions moved on too, leaving behind them many stories and many happy memories.

Left:
Simon Bolton and Oliver Dicks in conversation at the old bar in The Crown before alteration.
Right:
Oliver and Simon (left) watch landlord John Champion as he opens a bottle.
Photographs by Keyna Doran.

In the Public Interest

Opposite:
Northwick Bowling Club, showing the recent addition of a machinery shed on the right. Oliver also prepared the drawings for the extension to the left of the main clubhouse that is just visible.

"I could always phone him for advice on where to go for building and electrical work. He would tell you if you were talking nonsense. I would not have bought The Coach House without his say so."

Village clubs, societies and other community enterprises that had property among their assets inevitably turned to Oliver when contemplating alterations or extensions.

Northwick Bowling Club is one such entity. For a brief period in the early nineteen eighties Oliver was a member of the club along with Alan Savery[20]. On three occasions the club turned to Oliver to help it with plans for extensions. The first extension was to house a new men's changing room at the north-west end (the left-hand side when looking towards the clubhouse). This was a simple extension, although the planners insisted that the front of the extension was set back about 30 centimetres from the rest of the building, presumably to preserve the symmetry of the original design.

A few years later, the club was able to build a new ladies' changing room with the help of a donation from the eminent legal scholar and historian Sir Thomas Skyrme who lived at Elm Barns. Oliver again produced the drawings. "We just asked him", recalls the club's treasurer and trustee Alan Cother, "and he would say 'Yes, I'll do that for you' but he never accepted any money for it."

The new changing rooms were constructed at the rear of the building (see illustration), allowing the main clubroom to be enlarged. "Carefully remove internal stud partitions", Oliver's instructions said, adding rather importantly: "It is essential that a prior inspection takes place to determine that these partitions do not afford support to existing roof structure."

A few years later, in 2000, the club was in need of a more substantial machinery store. This time Oliver designed a store with a stone finish, to be positioned to the right of the main clubhouse. The stone finish was specified to remove

Below:
Oliver's drawings (before the arrival of a computer) of the new ladies' changing room at the rear. The original exterior is shaded grey, and an earlier extension can be seen on the right.

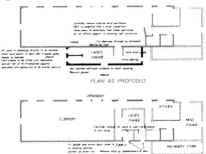

PLAN AS PROPOSED

PLAN AS EXISTING

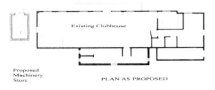

Above:
Oliver's drawing of the proposed machinery shed (left of picture) for Northwick Bowling Club

Opposite page:
The inner courtyard of Orchard Bank during an open day.
Below:
Oliver's drawings showing the plan to provide a covered vestibule and staircase to flats at Orchard Bank.

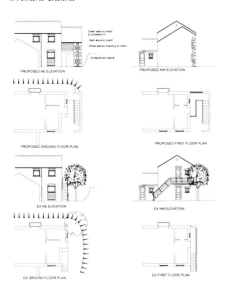

any fire risk as the store would be close to the existing timber building. The club was able to acquire the stone from the Sports & Social Club which had obtained a large quantity for its building purposes.

Although Oliver's active involvement in the game of bowls proved fairly short lived[21], he was invited to come to the clubhouse whenever he wished - as if he was an honorary member. So he would occasionally turn up for a pint on a Friday night or after a match. "A genuinely nice fellow" is how Alan Cother sums him up.

Orchard Bank

Oliver was also involved in another village project where Alan Cother was chairman. Midway along the High Street stands a relatively modern building known as Orchard Bank. It was established by the late Dr Jean Haine in 1964 as a place where the elderly may live in independent units of accommodation but under the overall oversight of a charitable foundation that looks after the property, provides regular communal meals and generally cares for the residents' interests.

In 1994 it became clear that access to one of the upstairs flats could be quite hazardous - especially on freezing winter days. The danger stemmed from the original design which provided access to the flat by means of an external concrete staircase that was exposed to all weathers. Oliver was called in to design some improvements that resulted in the building being extended to house an enclosed vestibule and staircase (see drawing).

Five years later problems were encountered with another upstairs flat. The staircase had been built from stones rescued by Dr Haine from Moreton in Marsh station. The only trouble was that they were laid incorrectly. To achieve the required height within the space available, the stones had been turned on their side so that the depth was narrower than the riser (height), making them very dangerous to descend. These steps too were exposed to the elements. So Oliver produced drawings for a replacement staircase, this time to be covered.

Jubilee Centre

Another public building to which Oliver devoted his expertise was the Jubilee Centre when it became clear that more storage space was needed to accommodate the amount of equipment being used by the playgroup. There was also a desire to provide disabled toilet facilities. Geoff Gregg, who was the parish clerk at the time, tells how the plans involved extending the existing hall by five

NORTH ELEVATION

Above:
Oliver's design for the proposed Heritage Centre that never became a reality. Instead there are plans to extend the Jubilee Centre (below right).

Below left:
Oliver's drawings for an earlier plan to extend the Jubilee Centre to provide more storage and a Parish Office above.

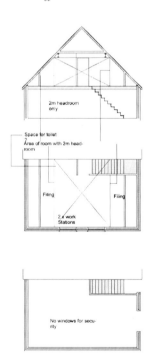

2m headroom only

Space for toilet
Area of room with 2m head-room

Filing   Filing

2 x work
Stations

No windows for security

metres towards the school, with double doors replacing the end window to give access to the new storeroom. Above the storeroom was to be an office for use by the parish council - as an archive, but also recognising that the council would not be able to rely indefinitely on a clerk using his own premises as a publicly available office venue. Access to the parish office would be by an internal staircase with door to the outside (just opposite the school kitchen entrance).

The area immediately beyond the entrance to the Centre would be incorporated into an enlarged toilet area which would include a disabled toilet. Oliver prepared detailed drawings. Unfortunately the plans were never implemented, although it is envisaged that a parish office will be included when the building is developed to include the proposed community heritage centre.

Oliver was involved in designing plans for an entirely new building to house the heritage centre before the opportunity arose to incorporate it into an enlarged Jubilee Centre. He took great trouble to create a building that would reflect traditional features of a Cotswold barn. Although the plan was put on ice when the development of the Jubilee Centre became a possibility, the drawings remain one more piece of evidence of Oliver's talent.

Another public works scheme undertaken by Oliver during Geoff Gregg's period as clerk was a plan for a bus shelter on Lower Street, set in to the dry stone wall opposite Mill View. Oliver did this when part of the wall had collapsed and bus routes had just changed with the Blockley central stop moving

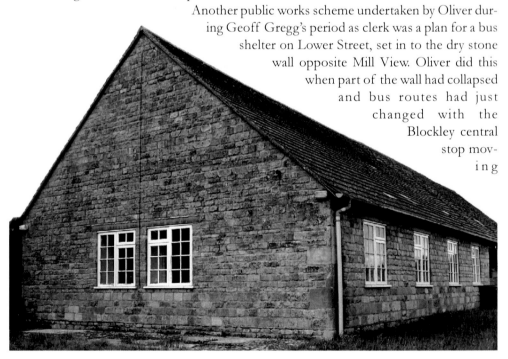

from the war memorial to Lower Street. Geoff recounts how an inset stone shelter "was a logical option to include in the wall repair".

Blockley Nursery School

Typical of Oliver's willingness to help the community is this account given by Sheila Weir. When her contract as a childcare consultant with Warwickshire County Council came to an end Sheila needed a new source of income and thought about opening a nursery school in Blockley.

The Old Coach House came on the market and Sheila asked Oliver to have a look at it. He considered it would be a sound purchase, but not worth the asking price. His advice was to get a good valuer to put a price on it. "Oliver was such a tower of strength", she recalls. "I could always phone him for advice on where to go for building and electrical work. He would tell you if you were talking nonsense. I would not have bought The Coach House without his say so."

Blockley Sports & Social Club

Blockley Sports & Social Club has been a thriving asset of the community for many years. It is situated on the road to Paxford on the way out of the village. When the club decided to create an area with a multi-sport artificial surface, there was a legal requirement to provide disabled access. So Oliver was called in to design it. "And it has been used", says vice chairman Marie Liptrot.

It may have been one of the smallest projects to which Oliver devoted his expertise, but his readiness to do so speaks volumes about the man.

Above:
The Old Coach House as it looks today. The Nursery School that Sheila Weir established occupies the top floor.

Below:
Oliver's drawing of the ramp leading to the multi-sport all weather surface at Blockley Sports & Social Club (left). The ramp (right) runs from the multi-sport pitches down to the pavilion seen in the distance.

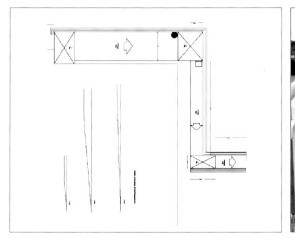 

CHAPTER 7

Trials and Tribulations

"Soon the emerging water was eroding the surrounding earth,
sucking it away from the house next door
and turning the entire site into a pond."

It would have been surprising, to say the least, if every project in which Oliver was involved had progressed smoothly to its conclusion. Building work has never been so simple. Couple that with the knowledge that Blockley has more than its fair share of brooks and underground springs and the scene is set for some exciting times.

The plan to extend Vine Cottage provides a good example. The building stands at the Dovedale end of the High Street immediately before Fish Cottage where a right-hand junction leads up to The Warren. At this point two tributaries to Blockley Brook converge. Many years ago the brook would have been fuller, but that was before Thames Water gained permission to pipe away a substantial quantity of water from a pumping station one hundred yards or so up stream. Nevertheless this continues to be a location where water and nature can combine to create a crisis.

Di Miller and Ade Louvain bought Vine Cottage in 1997. Together they run Di's professional photographic business in London and come to Blockley to relax. Di enjoys gardening and soon after the purchase she was allowed to cultivate a small part of a plot adjacent to the cottage. The plot was owned by one of the popular village doctors Frank Haine and when he died his heirs sought planning permission to develop the site, but without success.

Di and Ade grabbed the chance to buy the land, offering them the opportunity both to extend their cottage and to provide a seriously bigger garden. The existing cottage comprised only two bedrooms and two small reception rooms. Not surprisingly Di and Ade found this constrained their desire to entertain friends, given the social life that pervades every corner of Blockley.

Opposite page:
Vine Cottage with the new extension on the right.

92

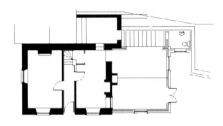

Above:
The proposed ground floor plan of Vine Cottage with the original external walls shaded black.

Below:
Oliver's drawings showing Vine Cottage before the refurbishment (left) and the proposed extension (right).

But most importantly they were attracted to the idea of a new project - one that they could plan and create themselves. Having acquired the additional land, Oliver was the natural person to produce drawings and obtain planning consent.

"Ollie was the first person we had contacted when we bought Vine Cottage", Ade explains. On realising that the roof needed repair, the previous owner Phil Cox had one simple recommendation: "Phone Ollie Dicks."

At the time they had no idea what Ollie did and assumed that he was probably a local builder. They were quickly disabused of that assumption. In Blockley people contacted Ollie Dicks because he knew everything about, and everyone involved in, building. But building was not something he actually did.

The design of the extension involved the usual debates. Oliver planned the bathroom to be at the back and it took a lot of persuasion before he relented to Di and Ade's desire to put it at the front. And they had to "fight like mad" to have a fireplace in the lounge. By now it will have become all too clear that Oliver could be very firm in his views, but as Di says: "He was always ready to acknowledge a better outcome than the one he had advocated."

The building work started in 2002. Alan Warburton was the builder and he was soon directing a digger to clear the area. Towards the rear of the site the digger made a deep incision into the soil with disastrous consequences. "Oh dear, we think we've hit a spring", Warburton reported.

Soon the emerging water was eroding the surrounding earth, sucking it away from the Fish Cottage garden next door and turning the entire site into a pond. "Passers by thought it might be a swimming pool", Ade recalls.

Worried about the impact on adjacent property foundations, structural engineer Peter Hemmings was called in to erect sheet piling. It successfully stopped the earth from moving, but not the water. However, sufficient stability had

Previous front elevation

Proposed front elevation

been achieved to allow work to resume on the site.

The next challenge was to design foundations that would be sufficiently safe for the extension. Twenty three piles had to be driven deep into the ground, each 150mm in diameter. Then a 300mm thick reinforced concrete floor slab had to be placed on top, covering 35 square metres.

One day, while digging out the ground for these piles, to everyone's amazement all the surrounding water suddenly disappeared within 15 minutes. The builders had struck an old drainage culvert and were thereafter able to pipe the spring water away. Di and Ade reckoned they deserved that lucky break, given how much anxiety and extra cost had preceded it: "It had been the most terrible time in our lives", Di recalls with obvious feeling.

So where was Oliver during this dramatic saga? He never took on the architectural oversight or project management role to the extent that would be expected in a more conventional client relationship. After all, his drawing work was free and arguably in such circumstances it would have been unfair for him to have to take responsibility for the construction implications on site. So he took a step backwards. However, as soon as the water problem had been overcome, he took a more active interest again. According to Di, he was very good after that: "He would phone us in London with reassuring progress reports, telling us that things were 'looking great'."

Phil Dunn took over the building contract after the flood, the extension was completed and now it has weathered to blend with the original cottage. So what are Di and Ade's reflections on Oliver's contribution? Di credits him with giving her "so much enthusiasm for building". Ade's recollection is more commercial. In common with many others, he found Oliver's cost estimating more than a little awry: "Hopeless…he could not price anything!" But they remain well pleased with what they created although, with all the water problems, the project took much longer than expected and cost much more. As Ade puts it: "We are both indebted to Oliver for his time and all his hard work. And we shall be eternally grateful for the whole of his contribution to what we consider to be the fine Cotswold house that we love."

Bridge Cottage

Bridge Cottage is a fairly modern house built in about 1965 and situated in Mill Lane. It looks down on the stretch of Blockley Brook that flows between The Old Mill and Mill Dene. Like most people in Blockley, the owners of Bridge Cottage - James and Alison Hunt - got on well with Oliver and liked him

Below:
Bridge Cottage overlooks Blockley Brook in Mill Lane.

a lot, so he was the obvious choice to draw up plans for an extension. But there were a few heart-stopping moments during the construction. At one stage there were fears that it would not be possible to get into the master bedroom because the levels were not correctly aligned. And then there was the occasion when the planning officer arrived for a site visit and asked James Hunt if he could explain how they had acquired an extra room in the basement. Apparently there had been a breakdown in communications between the builder and the planners.

Sunrise Cottage

It's one thing to embark on a house extension project that hits nasty problems along the way. It's another thing entirely to buy a property that self-evidently has structural problems from the outset. And that's exactly what Robert and Anna Stamp did.

Sunrise Cottage stands on the right-hand side of The Greenway on the way out of the village. For some years it was the subject of conversation among passers-by who noticed a vertical crack in the rendering on the front wall. Even passing cars would slow down, perhaps anticipating that Blockley was in an earthquake zone and expecting to witness a major collapse at any moment.

Robert Stamp admits that the footings "were not ideal", comprising just three courses of brick on a clay base. And the floors upstairs were all uneven. But the Stamps bought the property with their eyes open and with the experience that Robert brought to the task after graduating from Brunel University with a degree in building engineering and working in the building services industry for over 20 years.

Having first arrived in Blockley in 1994, the Stamps had bought Park Place in Park Road where they lived with daughter Jessica. Then Matthew was born and before long they were feeling the need for more space and some off-street parking. So they started looking around. They spotted Sunrise Cottage in 2003, late in the sale process, only to find that a buyer was already in negotiation with the owner. Shortly afterwards they noticed the "For Sale" sign had been taken down. So it came as something of a surprise to receive a phone call on the following Monday enquiring whether they were still interested.

"We knew it was not in a good state of health, but that it would keep us in the village", Robert explains. Within a week he had drawn up some plans, gained support from his bank and obtained a tentative response from the Council planning department.

The house had been built fairly cheaply in the early nineteen fifties as a week-

Above:

The front of Sunrise Cottage before alteration.
The earlier extension was to the left where the
roof line rises.

Below:

Oliver Dicks' designs for Sunrise Cottage
showing (to the right of the top drawing) the
rear window he created and (below) the
redesigned front of the property with the gable
and extended roofline above it.

EAST ELEVATION

FRONT ELEVATION

end cottage with tiles and bricks that are thought to have been sourced locally from Northcot Brick. Some 20 years later the property was extended to provide a double garage and additional bedroom accommodation above.

So how stable was the building? Robert engaged structural engineers to conduct a survey. They concluded that the cracking and movement in the wall stemmed from the extension work carried out in the nineteen seventies when part of the original side wall had been removed and the wall that remained above the first floor level had needed to be supported by beams and a pillar. The engineers' report said that this would have put an extra load on the front corner of the property, causing the movement to take place. The situation was compounded by seasonal variations in ground moisture that would have prompted some foundation movement because of the shallow depth of the footings.

For Robert Stamp this represented an interesting technical challenge to address, rather than something to fear. There was nothing inherently wrong with the site itself. To move matters forward, he would need help from someone who could prepare plans with sufficient knowledge and experience to ensure they would gain planning consent, and who could communicate with planners in an informed manner.

While talking about his plans with a friend Chris Jury, the name of Oliver Dicks was mentioned and an introductory meeting was set up at *The Great Western Arms*. "It soon became clear that Ollie knew what he needed to look at", Robert recalls. "We would then spend a couple of hours at a time in his study knocking around ideas on his computer. From what I saw of his work I could see that he knew what he was doing."

Robert thought it was ironic that Oliver retired from his position in building control because computers were taking over, only to discover how useful computers could be in designing alterations to existing properties.

Oliver suggested a number of features that were incorporated into the plans. They included the creation of a new staircase at the rear with windows that followed the shape of the staircase, decreasing in height in proportion to the height of each stair. He suggested introducing a gable at the front that would be mirrored at the rear, giving space for an additional bedroom while enhancing the overall appearance of the house. And he designed the roofline to mitigate the visual impact of the higher floor level adopted for the original extension to accommodate the rising hillside.

Which of Oliver's design contributions do the Stamps appreciate most? "The rear window and staircase", Robert replies. "It used to be very dark inside."

"His obvious love of buildings showed in his work - he loved detail", Robert adds, citing as an example the way Oliver took the specifications for the Crittall windows that Robert had researched and then worked them up into detailed drawings suitable for submission to the planners. Robert had great confidence in Oliver's reputation and the influence this would have on the planning department: "When the planners received plans from Ollie Dicks, you knew you were half way there."

But the Stamps and Oliver did have one difference of opinion. Oliver wanted to retain the curved bay window, but Robert and Anna favoured a square shaped bay. Oliver conceded. Once the plans had been submitted, Robert decided to telephone the council a couple of weeks before a decision was due in case the planners needed any further input. To his delight he was told the plans had gone through the committee without dissent. When, at a later date, it became necessary to extend the kitchen area by a further six inches, the planners had no objections to that either.

With his background in building services, Robert was happy to act as project manager, dealing with all the trades people. The family moved into the garage part of the property where they were to camp for many months while many of their possessions were stored in one bedroom upstairs. The first priority was to get the steelwork designed for the roof. Oliver recommended the use of civil engineering consultant Mike Carty to advise on this and on other structural implications of the planned alterations. Mike had been engaged previously on many of Oliver's other Blockley projects.

The next task was to underpin the foundations at the left-hand corner of the original building. Building control officers had imposed a requirement to go down two meters below ground level because the clay in the subsoil had broken into sand. As the builders dug out the soil for the footings adjacent to where the under-pinning was required, the corner of the building began to collapse. In due course, all the inherent structural problems were rectified and the building is probably now a lot stronger than most others.

In the Stamps' view, Oliver's great strength was his ability to stand back from the job and see what was required. As Robert puts it: "He had great patience and enjoyed working out all the details, but he was always happy to take a step back."

And his strongest memory? "Walking up to Ollie's front door, seeing him sitting up in his study, head down, looking at his computer screen." It is a memory that many will share.

Below (top to bottom):
Ground floor of Sunrise Cottage at the time of purchase, with previous extension shown shaded (top); Oliver Dick's drawing for the ground floor improvements (centre); Oliver Dicks' plan for enlarging the first floor (bottom).

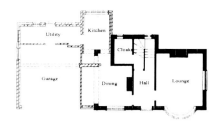

Ground floor before alteration

Ground floor after alteration

First floor after alteration

CHAPTER 8

Twentieth Century Transformations

*"He was always generous with his time, not only on building projects
but also in many other ways, like volunteering to take people to an
airport. He never charged a penny for anything."*

Not every Blockley property has its origins in the 17th or 18th century and Oliver was always willing to help people alter or extend their homes irrespective of when they were built. Melrose is a typical example. It stands on the left of Station Road as it leads away from the village towards Paxford, a little more than 100 metres from *The Great Western Arms*.

Melrose was built in 1930 using stone removed from part of Dovedale House after it had been ravaged by fire. Dovedale House had been the birthplace of the benevolent Blockley landowner Captain Edward George Spencer-Churchill[22]. The fire destroyed one wing completely and so there was plenty of stone available - much of it stained with reddish scorch marks.

Peter and Betty Mansion bought Melrose in 1998. It wasn't in very good condition and their immediate desire was to update it. In particular they wanted to create a utility room and add an en-suite bathroom at the rear of the property. As Peter recounted in his tribute[23], he met Oliver within a few days of arriving in Blockley. On Oliver's advice the builders were instructed to buy old stone and burn some of it for the Melrose extension to match the original derived from Dovedale House.

By 2004, the Mansions had decided they would like to replace their single detached garage with a double one. This seemingly simple intention soon evolved into something rather more substantial: "Ollie and I cooked the whole thing up one night in *The Great Western*", Peter recalls. "We thought we would put a room on top as well, creating a two storey building."

The new garage would need to be much lower than the house to allow ease of access from the road. And to avoid excessive foundation work, it would need

Opposite page:
How Melrose looks today
Below:
Oliver Dick's plan for extending Melrose

FRONT ELEVATION (SE)

Above (left to right): The rear of Melrose during initial extension works; Digging out the footings for the new garage and first floor extension above; Concrete beams link the existing house to the extension; Foundations being prepared for the garage and first floor extension.

Opposite page:
Cotswold Cottage in the winter sunshine .
Below:
Do-it-yourself - Peter Mansion exposes an original fireplace in Melrose.

to be located about four metres from the main house. Then Oliver had a brainwave. Why not link the two buildings with a conservatory-style structure, allowing the ground floor of the house to lead straight through to the first floor accommodation above the garage?

There was one technical challenge - the absence of any foundations for the linking structure. So Oliver suggested the conservatory should be slung between the two buildings on concrete beams.

Oliver progressed the planning application and dealt robustly with various requests from the conservation officer. Such requests were somewhat surprising bearing in mind that only the garden wall at the front of the property is within the village conservation area. One council proposal was that it would be "more in keeping" if a central pillar were to be erected between two garage doors, a proposal that took little account of the difficulties this would create when manoeuvring vehicles into or out of the garage.

Reflecting on the project, Peter Mansion acknowledges the "huge amount" of engineering expertise required to add a building at a different level and join the two together: "Ollie was unceasingly imaginative and always willing to go away and readdress an issue."

Cotswold Cottage

Arriving in Blockley from Bourton on the Hill, the principal road takes a sharp turn to the right at what is called Tally-Ho Corner while a secondary road proceeds straight ahead down to Mill Dene and the Blockley Brook. At the junction of these two roads stands a house known as Cotswold Cottage that was built in 1932 and is conspicuous for its lack of Cotswold characteristics.

The house was built with brick rather than Cotswold stone. That might not

Right:
Oliver's drawings of Cotswold Cottage from the rear, showing the previous and proposed elevations on the right of the building.

Previous rear elevation

Proposed rear elevation

Below:
Oliver's drawing showing the plans for the ground and first floors of Cotswold Cottage.

Additional bedroom

First Floor

Study

Ground Floor

have been very surprising, given the nearby Northcot Brick works that was founded by Captain Spencer-Churchill after the First World War[24]. But the bricks did not come from Blockley.

Between 1999 and 2009, Cotswold Cottage was home to John and Joan Dewhurst. By the time they bought the property they were already very close friends with Oliver and Jean Dicks, having been neighbours when both families lived in Northwick Terrace[25]. John first met Oliver at *The Crown* and they soon became regular drinking companions.

John tells the story of the occasion when he and Oliver were drinking quietly in *The Crown* at about 11 o'clock in the evening when the village policeman came in. "What shall we do?" enquired John, anxious about after-hours drinking. "Just follow me", Oliver replied.

"Are you still serving?" the constable asked. "Only friends", the publican replied. "I hope you count me a friend", said the constable, placing his helmet on the bar, "I'll have a pint please." Oliver bought the drink, as so often he did.

A year or two after moving into Cotswold Cottage, John and Joan were wanting more space. "I was fed up with John having his study in our bedroom", says Joan. "I said I wanted my bedroom back!" So they thought about extending the house to provide a ground floor study. Above the study there would be an opportunity to build an extra bedroom and to add an ensuite shower room to the master bedroom.

"Well you *could* do that" was Oliver's immediate response on learning of the plan. "He would come along with drawings for us to discuss", John recalls. "One of Ollie's great strengths was that he had an eye for what an idea would look like in practice." Sometimes John and Joan would think they had had a bright idea, only to be told by Ollie that "It won't look right" which John says really meant "I'm not doing that for you". According to John, there was Ollie's way and there was the wrong way.

Once planning permission had been obtained, two obstacles remained. First, a supply of matching bricks was required. Oliver and the builder Alan Warburton succeeded in sourcing the bricks with a little help from Northcot Brick. The second obstacle was the foul weather: having dug out the footings, by the following day they were full of snow. Later it rained so much that the mortar was washed away before it could be of any use.

As noted elsewhere, once the plans had been drawn and approved, Oliver did not get involved in overseeing the detailed implementation. John's explanation is that Oliver didn't have the patience for that role: "But he was always there if you needed him. He was always generous with his time, not only on building projects but also in many other ways, like volunteering to take people to an airport. He never charged a penny for anything."

Pinner's Quarry

Towering above the Dovedale valley - with an enviable view across it - is a twentieth century house built on the edge of a disused quarry. It's called Pinner's Quarry and is located on the higher reaches of Donkey Lane. Since 1981 it has been home to Tony and Mariam Gilbert, but was originally built for Harry Yoxall in 1939. The land was bought from a trust administered by the Spencer-Churchill and Bathurst land-owning families and came with a very particular condition: the building bricks had to be bought from the brickworks that Captain Edward Spencer-Churchill had established next to Blockley railway station to provide new employment opportunities after the closure of the Blockley mills .

Although the deeds refer to "Harry" Yoxall it seems this was the person known always as Henry Yoxall who had arrived in Blockley from Birmingham in 1919 after buying land and building a house for himself elsewhere in the village[26]. If that is the case, it must be assumed that he built Pinner's Quarry 20 years later for his son and daughter-in-law Ivan and Jona. The Yoxall's connection with Birmingham has been preserved in the form of a stained glass window which is thought to have been bought by the Yoxalls from King Edward VI School in Birmingham when its New Street premises were abandoned as a fire risk in 1936 and were subsequently demolished. The window has been incorporated into the Pinner's Quarry entrance hall and a small inscription identifies its source. It may be more than a mere coincidence that Henry Yoxall's daughter Nora became an accomplished artist in stained glass[27].

The Gilberts' first task was to clear the overgrown garden and carry out essential refurbishments to the house. This included the installation of central

Opposite page:
Pinner's Quarry after completion of the ground floor extension. Note the use of local bricks.
Right:
Oliver Dick's drawings of the front elevation before and after the ground floor extension.

EXISTING EAST ELEVATION

PROPOSED EAST ELEVATION

heating and redecoration . More notably, three dormer windows and a gable roof were added to provide additional accommodation for their family.

By 2003 they were eager to extend the ground floor to provide a breakfast room, an entrance porch and more storage. And while earlier modifications had not required planning consent, the new extension would do so. It was not difficult to decide where to turn for help. Oliver and Jean Dicks were already well known to the Gilberts, not least because Jean had catered for some of their parties and Oliver had been there to help. Tony and Oliver also shared a common interest in sports cars.

"How do you charge?" asked Tony. "I've retired", Oliver replied. "I only work for people I like. I don't take money, but I do like red wine…"

The Gilberts were keen to ensure that the proposed extension would retain the character of the existing building. So they decided it should have a pitched roof. However, this would have interfered with the light available to the first floor bathroom. To overcome this, Oliver designed the roof with a pitch on the outside behind which was concealed a flat roof (see drawing).

Like many others, Tony Gilbert was soon impressed by Oliver's expertise. The structure of the roof was quite complicated and Oliver revelled in designing it. Without being asked he would also calculate potential heat loss and the thickness of cavity foam required, and then suggest where to put the radiators. "His knowledge of building materials was encyclopaedic", Tony says, although little knowledge was required to source the bricks for the extension. They had to match the originals, both in colour and in their distinctive shape. A visit to the Blockley brickworks - by then renamed Northcot Brick - was all that was required.

The construction work was not without its challenging moments. The overhead power supply cable had to be re-routed underground and Oliver com-

Below:
Oliver Dick's floor plan for the Pinner's Quarry extension.

PROPOSED GROUND FLOOR PLAN

pleted all the forms required to facilitate this. The foundations had to be re-dug to satisfy the building inspector. And when the temperature dropped below 4°C the concrete mixing had to be delayed and the workmen sheltered indoors until it was warm enough to proceed. Despite these minor setbacks, the extension was completed successfully in May 2004.

While the work was under way Oliver declined Tony's request to come and check on the builders' progress: "I haven't got time to do that", Oliver explained, perhaps reflecting his reticence to take ultimate responsibility for something he had designed as a favour. Nevertheless he was always available to answer any queries that arose.

"He was a perfectionist", Tony recalls. "He had become such a part of the village fabric and had got to know all the people he could wish to work for and trust. For them he always made time."

North End House and Luke House

Towards the north end of the village is an area known as The Landgate and several properties in that location were to come under the design influence of Oliver Dicks. The Landgate leads off the right hand side of Park Road on the way out of the village towards Broad Campden, shortly after passing the junction with Greenway Road. The first property on the left-hand corner of The Landgate is North End House which for 30 years was home to the Jeffrey family until they decided to build a new house next door called Luke House. Oliver became involved in both.

After Luke House had been completed in 2007, Cotswold District Council took exception to some deviations from the plans that had been approved in

Below (left to right) :
Front view of North End House with the wall of Luke House on the right. Ground floor plan for North End House with extension shaded in grey. First floor plan for North End House extension.

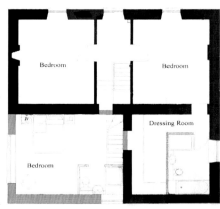

October 2002. "The completed dormers do not match the approved plans", the Council said. But that wasn't all. The Council's complaint went on to say that the external joinery, chimney details and slab levels specified in the planning permission had not been complied with. The verdict: "The current dwelling is therefore unlawful". In order to regularise the situation the Council recommended that a new planning application should be submitted to "seek the retention of the dwelling as built".

Oliver helped with the new planning application in October 2007. This succeeded in satisfying the planners and restoring the new house to legitimacy.

Meanwhile the Jeffreys had found a buyer for North End House in none other than Mark and Shirley Penfold who were looking to move from Meadowbrook[28] because they had "got bored and wanted another project". They were eager to create a self-contained annexe within the existing structure as a place for use by friends and family. So in November 2007 they called on Oliver to see how the floor plan might be modified for this purpose.

The proposed alterations could be readily achieved within the existing structure because a two-storey addition had been built on the north side in the nineteen seventies to fill in the fourth square of what had previously been an L-shaped structure. No planning consent would be required because the building was not listed. "Ollie and I measured everything up between us", Mark recalls. Oliver produced plans that would create a self-contained apartment with access to both floors from an existing external doorway. A kitchen and living area would be located on the ground floor and a new staircase would be introduced leading up to the first floor bedroom and bathroom. The core of the existing house would remain unaltered, apart from providing an en-suite bathroom and dressing room accessed from the master bedroom.

Having provided the drawings, Oliver withdrew while the work was done. Mark engaged the necessary personnel from the people he knew in the building trade and also worked on the project himself. "I don't want to see it until it is completely finished!" Oliver exclaimed. And that was how it was to be. Oliver and his wife Jean were invited to a celebratory dinner afterwards.

Cherry Orchard and Cadley Cottage

Robert "Budgie" Cadle had known Oliver Dicks for a long time before he and his wife Marilyn bought Cherry Orchard in Greenway Road in 2007. They first met in the early nineteen seventies - probably in a pub. Later Budgie moved from Park Road to Chipping Campden, but they remained good friends. "I had

Below:
Oliver Dicks' drawing of the Cherry Orchard's ground floor showing rear extension shaded in grey.

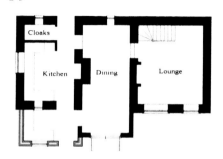

Proposed Ground Floor

Opposite page:
Cherry Orchard (left) and Cadley Cottage (right).
Right:
Oliver Dicks' drawings of the rear of Cherry Cottage before and after alterations.

Ex South Elevation

Proposed South Elevation

All window frames in natural oak

some fun with him", Budgie muses. That "fun" included flying in Budgie's Jodell 117D plane and seeing his beloved Blockley from a different perspective. It also extended to having friendly arguments, often prompted by one of Oliver's favourite retorts: "I'm sorry to say this but I'm afraid you're wrong!"

Budgie confesses to being something of a project addict, whether assembling motor bikes, shipping a Stolp Starduster aircraft in parts from the United States and reassembling it here, or rebuilding houses. Inevitably Oliver would be called upon when property projects were involved. So when Cherry Orchard came on the market, with planning permission to build a new house alongside it, the development challenge coupled with the opportunity to return to Blockley were too good to miss.

It was not long before Oliver was being asked for an opinion. "He was up here straight away", Budgie remembers. And Oliver's first comment was: "We'll get rid of that b...... mess up there!" That "mess" was a first floor extension to the rear of the cottage that Oliver had designed for previous owners but which had been constrained on cost grounds. Oliver had never liked it.

Plans were drawn up to modify the rear of Cherry Orchard and to refresh the property generally - to make it "more liveable". The previous extension would be modified to a more attractive two-storey gable roofed design, with French doors on the ground floor. Alongside it a utility room would be constructed with a new back door. Much of the interior would be upgraded with extensive use of light oak timber. "Come up home", Oliver said, and within an hour and a half he had produced the plans.

By the summer of 2008 the modifications to Cherry Orchard had been completed. Attention then turned to the bigger challenge of building the new house alongside. The previously approved design would have resulted in the property being set further back from the road beyond the line of the existing buildings.

As a result it would have interfered with the view from *Greenways* - the next house up the hill owned by John and Jan Humphreys. So the Cadles suggested to Oliver that the plans should be revised to reposition the property nearer to the road and to lower its height.

They measured up the garden and decided they could achieve their objective by making the house slightly smaller. "Oliver started drawing straight away", Budgie recalls. "And he sorted all the planning."

Meanwhile Marilyn and Budgie set about removing 700 tonnes of soil from the site and, with help from their son Justin, built retaining walls using 300 concrete blocks back-filled with 22 tonnes of concrete.

Once the plans had been approved, work started on the construction of the new property itself. Budgie employed two builder acquaintances to carry out the work, and the electrical work was carried out by Justin. The floor was constructed from pre-formed reinforced concrete beams and Oliver produced the detailed drawings to show where these should be positioned as well as where the damp-proof membrane should be located.

"He kept hassling us to get the drawings done", Budgie recalls. "He was really really good." Unfortunately Oliver died before the project could be completed. "He ran off and left us to finish it", Marilyn adds sadly. "He was no longer around to do the calculations, but we learned lots and lots and lots."

Hollybrook

Over the years the Blockley Brook has proved a magnet to househunters and developers alike. So it should come as no surprise to find a couple of relatively modern properties overlooking the brook, downstream from The Old Mill in Mill Lane. One of those is Hollybrook. It was bought by Maggie Taylor and Carl Murray in November 2002. But it was hardly big enough to accommodate a family of two adults and two teenage children with "very large friends", as Maggie puts it. "There were two bedrooms and a box room. We wanted a family house."

Oliver had been involved with the property's previous owner and already had some drawings, so he was the natural person to turn to. And anyway, as Maggie says, "you didn't go anywhere else".

Oliver devised a plan that would result in four double bedrooms, a large family bathroom and a "gorgeous" ensuite bathroom. Downstairs the kitchen and lounge were opened up to provide a walk through environment. And an additional sitting room was created in the space previously used as a garage.

Opposite:
The view along Mill Lane with Blockley Brook flowing along both sides. Two properties have been built overlooking the brook - Hollybrook (below) is just out of view to the right of the picture. Beyond it and just visible behind the trees is Bridge Cottage (see page 95). Oliver helped design alterations to both.

Right:
The floor plan of Hollybrook before and after
Oliver redesigned it.

Existing

Proposed

Ground floor   First floor   Ground floor   First floor

Below:
Hollybrook from the rear before and after
Oliver redesigned it. Note the new glazed void
in the centre and the enlarged footprint of the
left-hand wing.

But the best feature of all was conceived by Oliver. The existing entrance hall extended upwards to the top floor which was accessed by an open staircase. Oliver suggested extending this two-storey void through to the back of the house with a glazed roof at the rear and fold-back doors leading out to the garden patio. It transformed the ambience of the house into something far more roomy and airy. The upstairs landing was converted into a catwalk linking both sides of the house - an idea possibly borrowed from his work on The Old Chapel (see chapter 3).

The planners agreed to the extensive use of glazing on this feature, but were less enthusiastic when Maggie thought she would like to install French windows leading from the kitchen to the garden too. That idea had to be abandoned.

One of the constraints on living space on the top floor was the narrowness of the rear wing with an unusually steep (and rather unattractive) pitch of roof above it. Oliver came up with what Maggie regarded as a very clever idea - he suggested widening the footprint of the wing and in doing so the roof pitch would also be made more shallow. That provided enough room to create a family-size bathroom and to convert the box room into a double bedroom. What's more, it didn't need any more roof tiles.

Conversations between Maggie and Oliver would often be punctuated with the request: "Could you show me...?" At this Oliver would head home to his computer and, within what seemed like minutes, he would return with a drawing. "And if we didn't like it, he would go off and draw something else", Maggie recalls. "He was strong-minded about his ideas, but ready to respond to another suggestion. He was always creative, always fast and a wee bit stubborn."

Smaller projects

Not all of Oliver's design projects were extensive in their scope. Often he would be asked to produce drawings to support a planning application for outbuildings like the conservatory for Bruce and Rosemary Idiens at Orchard House off Chapel Lane and a field shelter for Jeremy and Ann Bourne at Malvern Mill. He even designed a cycle rack for use at a flat in Oxford owned by Blockley's Richard Bates: "Within minutes and a lager later, he produced a drawing." On other occasions, Oliver simply came to the aid of neighbours, like helping Bob and Pat Drysdale reconfigure the inside of Greystones.

When Sheila Weir realised that, with oncoming osteoporosis, she would eventually need a bathroom on the ground floor of her Wold Cottage, Oliver's response was predictable and immediate: "Let me come up with my tape measure." Sheila decided that, if she was going to extend the ground floor, she would also like a little porch. "I gave Oliver my ideas and he re-jigged them. I couldn't believe how much he could get into an area that was just two metres wide - an ensuite upstairs, cloakroom and utility room downstairs, plus a porch!"

In 2003 Caroline and Austen Gee found they needed more space after moving into one of the new houses in Mill View, overlooking Blockley Court, with their two year old son Daniel. Explaining their predicament to Oliver during Saturday lunch at *The Great Western Arms*, the immediate response was: "Right, let's go and have a look!" Having arrived at the house, Oliver sent Austen to fetch his tape measure and camera. Within 20 minutes Oliver had measured up and taken all the details he needed. Forty-eight hours later he reappeared with plans. In due course Oliver would describe his proposal in the planning application accurately, but with masterly understatement, as "a small extension to existing porch". The so-called extension would provide a utility room and a much larger entrance lobby to accommodate boots, pushchair, car seat and all the other paraphernalia that follows the arrival of young children. It would also make room for a tumble dryer and a fridge-freezer.

So how big was the porch before? It was no more than an inverted "V"

Below (left to right):
The porch style at 3 Mill View that was subjected to a "small" extension by Oliver; the enlarged floor plan; the property after completion of the extension.

fitted above the front door (see photograph). It offered an aesthetically pleasing touch to the property, but little if any protection. The description caused the council planning officer mild amusement on visiting the property, but planning consent went through unchallenged.

The site for the extension was so small that there was no room for a mechanical digger. Instead the builder Alan Warburton had to dig the foundations by hand and was not best pleased when the building inspector insisted they should go deeper than he had intended. But the finished product was a great success. The tiles and stones were distressed to match the existing ones and within six months no-one would have known there had been an extension. "It looks better now than before", says Austen. "People commented on it as 'a brilliant job'."

Predictably Oliver took no reward for his efforts. Such was his generosity that he even offered the use of his red Vauxhall Nova after Austen had written off his own car on his way home from visiting Caroline in hospital.

There were other times too when Oliver simply came to the rescue of a friend in need, as illustrated by this account of the occasion when Arthur and Beryl Godfrey were moving into Pinner's View in Days Lane. It was February 1987 and the village was under snow:

"We arrived at noon to find the previous owners had not started to move out, so decided to go to *The Crown* for lunch and ran into Ollie whom we already knew. At about 4.30pm we returned to Day's Lane with some difficulty, accompanied by Ollie, to find the previous owners' removal team ripping out the last carpet from the lounge. In doing so they caught the radiator inlet pipe, leaving a spout of water gushing onto the floor as they left with a cheery wave.

"Being a practical type I stuck my finger over the pipe and asked Ollie where the hell I could get a plumber at 4.45pm on a Friday evening. 'Leave it to me', said Ollie, and some twenty minutes later he returned with Mike Johnson who

Below:
Nothing was too small for Oliver - Pinner's View at the top of Day's Lane (left), Greystones where he helped reconfigure the interior (centre), and the conservatory he added to Orchard House (right).

he introduced as the only plumber in Blockley. By 5.30pm the offending pipe had been reconnected and the flood of water into the lounge had ceased. I was left nursing a bruised finger that had been stuck in the pipe for the best part of an hour. With that task completed Ollie decided to go off to *The Crown*. I was never more grateful for having a knowledgeable friend at hand."

Some months later, the Godfreys decided they needed a second bathroom, but could not envisage where to fit it into their relatively small cottage. They put some ideas to Oliver, but the only reply they received was: "Absolutely no chance!" Nevertheless he offered to seek a solution which he soon presented. "Suffice it to say that, having agreed to what *he* decided, we left it to him", Arthur Godfrey recalls. "He supervised the work, arranged the contractors and obtained whatever permissions were necessary. All we had to do was pay the bill and marvel at Ollie's brilliant brain that had managed to squeeze a quart into a pint pot."

Oliver's talent was employed again after the Godfreys sold Pinner's View to Paul and Pauline Blaikley in 2003. The newcomers decided it would be a good idea to transform what was then a rather dead grassed area beyond the house into hard standing for cars. Paul Blaikley remembers Oliver turning up almost instantly with his tape measure: "He had drawn up plans and submitted them for planning permission on our behalf almost before we knew it." Later, Oliver was also to provide valuable advice on the feasibility of installing a downstairs toilet and on reconfiguring the kitchen.

Woodlands

When toying with the idea of calling this book *Rebuilding Blockley* the title was not meant to be taken too literally. However, in one particular case the word "rebuilding" is entirely apt.

Shortly before reaching Dovedale Cottage at the far end of the High Street, a lane leads off to the right towards The Warren. Above that junction, looking

Below:
The previous Woodlands property (left);
Demolition in progress (centre); Oliver Dicks -
sitting on the left - looks on during the
demolition process (right).

Opposite page:
Woodlands nearing completion in its picturesque
autumn setting.

back along the High Street from its enviably elevated position, there used to be a house called Woodlands. It was a relatively modern, unprepossessing property. And "was" is the operative word.

Today an entirely new house stands on the site, designed by Oliver and owned by Alan ("Sarj") and Debbie Sarjant. They were among several people who had sought and bought the previous house hoping to build a new property there that would do justice to the site.

The Sarjants had moved into the village in 2006 seeking a bolthole from their workplace in Solihull. They would often spend a weekend in Blockley and feel reluctant to leave. So it will come as no surprise that their search for a more permanent and larger home centred on this village. "It's perfect for community and commuting", explains Debbie. "It had to be Blockley, and the heart of Blockley. It's 50 minutes from Sarj's office and I can work anywhere."

The Sarjants' initial interest in Woodlands waned as property prices continued to rise, and after a while they pulled out. But in due course this would prove to have been a significant benefit. They were able to observe the property throughout the summer, noting where it caught the sun and where it did not, witnessing the dramatic floods that invaded the village in July 2007 and deciding which part of the site was most suitable for an entirely new house. By the end of October 2007 prices were more favourable and so they bought the property.

Long before this, Oliver had heard of the Sarjants' interest in Woodlands. He had already done some drawings for the previous owners who had not proceeded with the development. One day he arrived at the Sarjants' door with those drawings in his hands. "This", he said firmly, "is the last site in Blockley." He explained that he was not committed to his first drafts and would be happy to develop them. The offer made immediate sense. As an industrial property developer, Sarj had some strong ideas. He could see that he would enjoy working with Oliver and would benefit from his exhaustive knowledge of Cotswold architecture. That seemed a lot better than using a big firm of architects who would have their own ideas and be hard to influence.

The overall aim was to create a traditionally styled Cotswold home. With Sarj and Debbie bursting with ideas, Oliver was happy to work with them on the detail such as the correct pitch for the roof. "Often Sarj would phone Ollie with an idea and by the afternoon he had drawn it!" Debbie recalls. "He was able to make use of his own extensive building experience and to combine it with the fruits of his very keen observation."

Such was Oliver's enthusiasm and commitment that he would drive Sarj and

Photograph: Debbie Sarjant

Debbie around local villages to look at features like window details or to talk to local craftsmen. On one occasion, Oliver suddenly diverted from the planned route towards a home whose owners had only moved in a week or so previously. "Hello Roger. I want to show these people round your house", Oliver announced. The detour became a long and happy evening that ended up in a local pub.

Design plans progressed slowly but the Sarjants had plenty of time. They were now renting in Solihull while Debbie's daughter took her A levels. The plan was to rent out Woodlands for six months and Oliver even helped to broker the deal. Paul and Julie Dove, who were realising Oliver's designs for Chapel Cottage, moved into Dovedale while their building work was being done.

One aspect of Oliver's original design was changed solely because of the knowledge gained by the Doves living in the old house. To maximise the impact of the morning sun, they decided to move the positions of the master bedroom and ensuite bathroom.

Inevitably Oliver's robust opinions came to the fore from time to time, such as when the Sarjants thought it would be a good idea to build a porch that went all round the house. "You can't do that!" was the unequivocal response. Oliver also objected to the use of "jumpers" - stones that are two courses high - in the construction of walls. "That's disgusting", he would say, using one of his most popular phrases. In the context of authentic Cotswold construction he was probably technically right. But as Debbie pointed out, there were far more "disgusting" things in the world: "He didn't mind you standing up to him. Sometimes he would simply laugh and give in. He never brought his own ego to the project."

Right:
The front elevation of Woodlands as drawn by Oliver Dicks

The initial plan had been to use stone mullions to frame the windows throughout the house. But that would have proved very expensive. So Oliver took the Sarjants to see examples of two alternatives using a steel casement - one set in a wooden frame and the other without. They agreed on wood and steel for most of the windows, the exceptions being two bays that have been set into stone mullions.

A similar dilemma arose when choosing the style of roof tile. Traditional stone tiles would have been costly, but Oliver introduced the Sarjants to concrete imitations that looked just like the real thing, made in multiple sizes to allow progressively smaller tiles to be used as they get closer to the top of the roof, in the traditional Cotswold manner. The tiles, called Cardinals, were made to look weathered and aged, and had been pre-approved for conservation area usage. As usual, Oliver knew someone who was using them and took the Sarjants to have a look.

Eager to ensure the new house looked as weathered and authentic as possible from the outset, a search began for reclaimed stone. Eventually Oliver was able to source about 70% of the required quantity from the old Oxford University physiology building. This was augmented by stone carefully matched from the local Stanleys Quarry and some beautiful reclaimed quoins.

Oliver's dealings with the planners taught Debbie a lot about how to work with them: "We had two or three pre-meetings with them, and carried out a geological investigation, tree survey and soil tests before submitting the plans."

Below:
The steel windows set in wooden frames that
Oliver Dicks and the Sarjants chose.

The pivotal moment arrived on Friday 25 July 2008, the day before the Sarjants were going on holiday. There had been no news from the planning department, so Oliver took the initiative and phoned them. Debbie sat in his little office in trepidation, listening to one end of the conversation and wondering what the planner was saying at the other end. After a while Oliver uttered the magic words: "They will be so happy." The plans had been approved.

When work started in October 2008, the first task was to demolish the existing building. Everyone had expected to see a wrecking ball in action, but instead the roof was removed and then the walls were given some fatal nudges by a conventional digger. Twelve minutes later everything had gone.

The first structural headache came with the need to build a retaining wall to hold back the hillside behind where the house would be built. The groundworkers dug straight down through the clay, fortunately with no major collapse and - unusually for Blockley - no evidence of springs. So far, so good.

But 10 days after erecting the retaining wall, it rained heavily and the wall

Right:
Building the retaining wall at the rear of the Woodlands site (left); Excavation and construction of the Woodlands basement area (right).

started to move. As a remedy, vertical steels from an old power station were driven into the ground. In between them were inserted lengths of concrete that previously had been crash barriers at the Silverstone racing circuit. Gabion stone-filled baskets were placed in front of the wall as a further precaution and concrete was used to infill behind.

The design of the house involved digging out a basement area beneath the house, providing more space without above-ground impact. Tons of black clay were excavated - some of which went to a village potter. But the transportation of the pre-cast basement panels to the site provided the hairiest moments of the build. Residents all along the High Street kindly moved their cars aside so that some massive vehicles could get by. Debbie remembers it all too well: "They were the two worst days of the project. We stood waiting in the rain for an 80-tonne crane to wind its way along the High Street."

Throughout the project Oliver was involved as much as he could be. He was there when the previous house was being demolished. He was there when the digging began. But he did not live long enough to see the house come out of the ground.

Debbie and Sarj look back with great appreciation: "He was a brilliant sounding board. He liked to work with people who were fun and not easily offended. He didn't need to spend so many hours on the project, but he was always going off to produce another drawing and looking for a positive response."

Debbie took some pictures of the new basement to show Oliver in hospital in Cheltenham the day before he died and he was offering practical advice till the last. "As I left, he gave me the thumbs up", she remembers. "He knew we'd see it through."

Yes, Woodlands certainly was what Oliver called "the last site in Blockley". It was also the last site in Blockley to benefit from his uniquely personal and irreplaceable contribution.

Notes and References

1. See page 58.
2. See *Blockley through Twelve Centuries* by H E M Icely, p224
3. See *Blockley through Twelve Centuries* by H E M Icely, p168.
4. See "Rock Cottage" pp 14-18.
5. See *Blockley through Twelve Centuries* by H E M Icely, p148.
6. According to the archivist at St James's School, Malvern, Mrs Judson's daughter Florence moved the school from Blockley to Malvern Link with the encouragement of Canon Houghton, the Vicar of Blockley who had himself moved to Worcester. By 1916 the school had moved to the Abbey at Malvern Wells. The Abbey merged in 1979 on to the St James's site. The Abbey itself is now an International College. St James and the Abbey were joined later by another Malvern girls' school Lawnside and then, in 2006, they joined with Malvern Girls College, on the Malvern Girls College site which was originally the Imperial Hotel from the hey day of the Malvern Spa.
7. The book was traced to the Grafton Bookshop in Canada and acquired for the Blockley Heritage Society.
8. See page 52.
9. See page 42.
10. When the Dicks family bought the property it had been named "Sleepy Hollow" because of its use in the film with that title. Later the name was changed by Sir Robert Lusty to "The Old Silk Mill" .
11. See page 7.
12. By this time Sir Robert Lusty had sold the property to the Usher family.
13. See page 8.
14. See page 8.
15. See page 92.
16. The photograph on page 63 also illustrates the roof line.
17. The story goes that US personnel regularly frequented *The Red Lion* - see also page 72.
18. Previously known as Blockley Antiquarian Society.
19. Based on research among files at Cotswold Distrct Council and recollections of Alan Bennett and Simon Bolton.
20. See page 47.
21. He joined with Alan Savery of the Saw & Bone Mill - see page 47.
22. See *Blockley through Twelve Centuries* by H E M Icely, p147.
23. See Chapter 1.
24. See *Blockley through Twelve Centuries* by H E M Icely, p152
25. See page 8.
26. Henry Yoxall built "Windywold" where Ian and Bridget Reekie now live - see *Blockley through Twelve Centuries* by H E M Icely, p157
27. Nora Yoxall lived for some time in the former *Red Lion* inn - see also page 72.
28. See page 65.

Index